Foreword

I have been writing since I was a little girl.

My personal journals span 40 years.

Hopefully, those who read this book will laugh or cry or get angry, yet enjoy the stories.

This book contains real stories and allusions to common fairy tales we know from our childhood. It speaks of dreams, passion, seeking and believing in living happily ever after.

Some people are storytellers. Some people listen to other's stories and analyze what they have observed. I am the later after all I am a Psychologist.

My motivation in writing this book is to reveal thoughts, emotions, fears and love in themes that most women share. I offer them so we can deal with these on our own terms.

My goal is to be the friend who will tell you stories and reveal truths you can relate to.

I have shared my personal stories and professional advice.

It will be an ideal "bedside companion".

I hope the reader will take and enjoy the journey!

Dr. Wendy James
(First Edition 2013)

Chapters

I. Passion 6
II. Givers and Takers: which one are you? 11
III. The rule of threes: My Sweetie Pie 14
IV. 100% Unconditional 19
V. Guys are the ultimate recyclers 24
VI. Virtue 28
VII. If I had a hammer, I wouldn't need a husband 35
VIII. Breakthrough 40
IX. Men are frogs women are princesses 43
X. Sex and Chemistry – otherwise he is just a friend 46
XI. How can I meet the right guy? 51
XII. Being in Love…... 55
XIII. The Fairy Princess and our desire as women 61
XIV. Every Girl Wants to be Special and to be noticed 67
XV. Do you wear your sexy underwear for you or your man? 74
XVI. My Princess Dress 77
XVII. And the worst feeling is I do not exist 81
XVIII. Active Participation 87

XIX. Mirror, mirror on the wall, who is the fairest of them all? 90

XX. What do you want to talk about? 93

XXI. Overcoming yourself 97
    Professional 98

XXII. Do you have a dog or a cat and are you single? 102

XXIII. Worry, worry, worry 105

XXIV. Women do not want to be rescued even though they want to be the Fairy Princess 110

XXV. Keep the fire ignited 114

XXVI. Communication or lack of Communication in a Relationship 120

XXVII. We all want Respect! 125

XXVIII. Take an adventure 129

XXIX. Blame it on the Venezuelans: It is their fault 133

XX. Small Steps to Success as Women…Rub their backs 138

XXXI. As Women, we are Strong 142

XXXII. Women Control the Relationship 144

XXXIII. Willpower, The Art of Self-Control 149

XXXIV. Trust: How do you recover from your husband having an affair? 152

XXXV. Divorce – the slow fading of your bond to each other 157

XXXVI. Getting Old Gracefully 167
XXXV. Dragged into Retirement 174
XXXVI. Commitment: Marriage is special and sacred 178

I. Passion

"Between men and women there is no friendship possible. There is passion, enmity, worship, love, but no friendship." - Oscar Wilde

Personal

Passion drives us into the arms of others, because without the sharing of our passion, what do we really have?

We women are willing slaves to our passions. It has always been so.

Better that we are willing slaves to our own passions than to have our passions supplanted or suppressed in favor of someone else's. At least, being willing slaves to our own passions, we control what is important to us.

True, we are driven to share our passions with others. This sharing increases the intensity of what we already possess. The question becomes, how can we share our passions and include our man in the fulfillment of them?

First, you have to realize you need to be immersed in love. Love is the catalyst to sharing and satisfying the pursuit of your passions. You have to commit to make it so with someone whom you can share it with over the years.

Occasionally, as single women, we attempt to convince ourselves that we are okay with a one-night stand. Yet, after that one night of passion has passed, don't we still wait by the phone for him to call? Do we eventually shrug our shoulders and tell ourselves that it was, after all, what we wanted? We are liberated women and it was just about sex, wasn't it? Still, in the back of our mind do we wonder why he didn't call?

After all, it was great, wasn't it?

Sometimes, passion overlaps with the romance. He makes that phone call. That is when we shiver at the thought of seeing him again. He makes us anxious with anticipation. We wear our sexy underwear under our sexy clothes or under our business suit just in case.

We twirl in front of the mirror to make sure the outfit is just so and put on that little extra bit of lipstick and mascara. We get excited when he calls to share his day with us and then asks us about ours. We cannot wait to see him for an evening of passion and romance.

The most wonderful time in my life is when I share the love and passion with the one who has love and passion for me. That is the moment when our individual passions intertwine.

Then, it is more than special. It is the best you can ever ask for. That combination of passion and love transcends the trials and tribulations of life and makes every moment worthwhile.

I am the girl who believes in the "knight in shining armor". I believe in the Cinderella story. I believe in the Fairy Godmother. I believe in romance, passion, wooing, flowers, dancing, diamonds and sexy clothes.

Professional

In a male dominated society women have always been a mystery.

We like it that way.

It is that irresistible allure that we, as women, have developed and perpetuated for millennia. That mystery has always helped us to level the social/sexual playing field, solidifying our place of power in society.

The question is can the "mysterious woman" solidify her place among her co-workers? We struggle with our relationship with our female co-workers as much as we struggle for our place among the men.

We need to be recognized by both.

To be accepted by women, we wear appropriate clothing, makeup, etc. We still compete with other women for our place in female society.

Girlfriends, be honest. We get dressed to the max when we are going out with our girlfriends.

From the time we were little girls, we have learned how to compete for the attention of men. We compete for dates and later for success in business.

We develop our own style. Our use of makeup and our choice of clothes complete our unique look and reflects who we are. It builds our self-confidence and persona.

Now the question is, how can we strip away the veils of mystery to gain our rightful place and recognition for our achievements?

We need to keep our personal life distinct from work. We need to be promoted for our abilities and accomplishments to feel accomplished.

As women, we struggle with balancing our various roles at work, at home, in marriage and with our children. We want to meet all the demands of running a household to be the best employer/employee, the best wife, the best mother and the best of friends.

Sometimes these multiple roles may lead us to the question, "could we have done better"? This can lead us into feelings of "guilt".

Guilt has been a legacy of generations of women. Girlfriends, we all know "guilt".

The universal feeling of "guilt", perpetrated by our mothers, is part of our inheritance. We continue to fight with these feelings.

As mothers and sisters, we continue on the same cycle of guilt we have tried to interrupt.

Girlfriends, guilt is a part of our female being. Awareness of it is half the battle.

Therefore, when we recognize we are experiencing that old feeling of guilt, we have the power to say, "Stop the madness. Stop the guilt", and go back to our caring nature.

Guilt is something unique to women. Men never seem to be troubled by guilt. Go figure.

Men may be sorry, remorseful or regretful, (for an amazingly brief period of time) but guilt is just not part of their lexicon.

Guilt is a female trait. We own it!

II. Givers and Takers: which one are you?

"My father said there were two kinds of people in the world: givers and takers. The takers may eat better, but the givers sleep better." Marlo Thomas

Personal

I am a giver and had to learn to be a taker, just for balance.

I discovered that I had a problem letting others take care of me. Maybe, that is why I chose to be a psychologist. I have the talent and inclination to listen and to give. It was a reason I was also a teacher.

I realized, when there is a lack of balance between giving and taking, it does not work.

The only person, who I have allowed to give to me, is my husband. It is important to have a balance of giving and taking. If not, a taker will focus on herself, giving nothing to a relationship.

For the giver, who takes nothing in a relationship, this lack of balance can result in feelings of isolation, alienation, emptiness and loneliness.

Professional

We, as humans, fall in to one of two categories. Either we spend our life, predominately, as a giver or as a taker.

Think about which you are?

Are you a person that seeks to give with no expectation of receiving in a relationship?

Is giving the most important aspect of your life?

If you are a giver, you have control over whom you seek as friends and as lovers. You get to decide which people will be your friends and reject others.

Takers have no power without a giver.

Girlfriends, we get to choose those with whom we want to have a relationship. We can choose whether to have relationships that consist of too much taking and not enough giving. At any point, if we are unhappy or unfilled, we can decide to severe the relationship.

It is problematic when one person is always the giver and the other is always the taker. Eventually, the giver will realize this one-sided relationship only works for a certain amount of time. The taker often uses up the giver and then moves on. If you always take, and never give, you have no investment in a relationship.

Girls are taught to fit in. From the time we were little, we wanted to be part of the group.

So often, it is the taker who indicates to the giver whether they are right for them.

The takers are the ones who have demands, who use their clout and their social prestige to collect followers, suitable givers.

Girlfriends, we grew up being influenced by others, who judged whether we're right for the "in" group. If not, we were rejected. The use of rejection or fear of rejection gave the takers control.

The flip side to this is the giver soon becomes resentful in this type of relationship, because after time, she feels she is not receiving anything rewarding in exchange.

What about you?

III. The rule of threes: My Sweetie Pie

"A kiss is a lovely trick designed by nature to stop speech when words become superfluous" - *Ingrid Bergman*

Personal

I taught my husband about the rule of threes. Girlfriends, we all know this rule.

If I say something three times, it is important!

My husband gets very focused, when he is solving a problem at work, and would tend to stay up late. I would come into the library room, where he was, and say, "Honey, time to come to bed".

Men may appear to not hear you. In reality, if they are not making eye contact with us or if we are talking and walking to another room, they either do not hear us, or choose not to.

The second time I'd go to the library, I'd dress in a sexy outfit and say, "Honey come to bed."

If I still got no reaction, the third time I'd go into the library naked and say, "Now it is time to come to bed". The third time is always the charm. He likes the enticement and he finally understands.

I have learned to let him "fix" things around the house. Sometimes, he even gets around to doing them. Men like to fix things, but not necessarily, on our timeline.

One example is when the fluorescent lights in our bedroom closet went out. It was dark and I had already asked him to change the bulbs three times. I finally said. "Honey, I cannot see my clothes to dress in the morning". So he left and went to the store. I expected him to come back with some fluorescent bulbs. Instead, he came back with a flashlight.

Again, men like to solve problems. They just don't solve them as we might expect.
He just bought himself another two weeks to change the light bulbs.

Needless to say, he had to call an electrician to change the fixtures from fluorescent to incandescent to make sure the bulbs were easier to change in the future.

His personal theory is that, when a light bulb goes out, they'll all go out in short order, so it is best to wait to change them all at once. After all, why go to the effort of pulling out the ladder to change one bulb?

I have learned that his process is different than mine, and he is my "Sweetie Pie"!

Professional

The sweetest words a girl can hear from her lover is him saying, "Hi, Sweetie Pie"!

We are pleasers and always will be pleasers, at least for the girls that want to be with a guy. We will sacrifice our careers, our personal adventurers and willingly exchange those for experiences together! That is what our wildest dreams are about – going out on an adventure with our mystery man, our lover, our friend and our "Sweetie Pie".

Girlfriends, listen up. If you make the time to be with your man, you can have both a career and a wonderful, fulfilling relationship.

Remember, he is now the reason we get up. He is the one with whom we want to share our day, our dreams and our successes. We used to get up for our job, our friends or our family. Now, it is for our man, our "Sweetie Pie".

We started this behavior as young girls. At the time, we never fully understood what was going on…we just knew that we were suppose to have a guy. We wanted to love a guy, yet we also wanted to have something that was just ours. Oh, my girlfriends, we wanted and still want it all!

Some girls say that they want to stay home, be pampered and taken care of. That is the furthest from the truth.

What we actually want is for someone to notice us. Girlfriends, we all want someone who looks at us to confirm we are sexy. We want a man in our life who needs and loves us as much as we need and love him.

What is so important about being together? Is it the caring, the sex or just doing something with your lover?

I watch many girls' reaction when they hear about a couple that is so "perfect" together. It almost seems threatening to them. They will deny, resent, envy and try to rationalize the "perfect" relationship. Yet, deep down they want what the other girl has, because we all want to be loved by a man. A man who loves us when we're sick, when we are sexy and when we're hurting or sad.

We want him to be a "guy-guy". We want him to look into our eyes and have desire. It is desire, not contentment or comfort that we are looking for. We can get comfort from our girlfriends or our dog.

Desire is that look in our guy's eyes that tells us we are special. We are the one he chooses. We are the one worth going to battle for. We are the one who is worth coming home to. We are the one who is the most important to him and we believe he is the most important person in our life.

Now, girlfriends, listen up! It is our job to continue to make sure our man is happy with us. In response, he makes us feel special. He fancies us over and over, day after day and year after year.

Yes, as women, we may occasionally fail in this area. The good news is the man is fine the next day, if we give him a glance, flirt, rub his shoulders, crawl into his lap for a hug, laugh or dance.

That is what we are looking for…to be special and loved.

So, girls, we need to realize the "Fairy Tale" is still there when we have romance, love and adventures with our guy. It is the "Happily Ever After" story.

We have to desire, pursue and fulfill our man's needs. It will be in returned in kind!

IV. 100% Unconditional

"Love is giving to another the ability to destroy you but trusting them not to" Dr. Wendy James

Personal

When I met my husband, I told him "I loved him" first. He said he "thought it first".

Afterwards, I said I would give 100%. How could he do any less? I mean he's a guy. Guys rise to a challenge.

I am still trying to give 100%. However, I discovered that a relationship is never 100%. It is never 50 – 50. It is never over 100% because you cannot give more than 100%. The reality is all you want from your man is to give you love and support and all he wants from you is to give him love and support too.

A perfect example of how men and women are different occurred when we invited another couple to accompany us on a wine tour of Napa Valley.

While visiting the Beringer Winery, we were educated on how different wines were blended to achieve a distinctive, unique taste. Then, we were invited to try our hands at blending our own wine, label it and then have a blind taste test to determine which wine was ours and which of the four was the wine we liked the best.

Both my girlfriend and I carefully measured and blended our individual wine exactly as instructed. When it came to labeling our wines, we chose names related to nature or just a catchy one.

When it came to the blind tasting, we girls could not distinguish our own wines from the others in our foursome.

On the other hand, our husbands generally ignored the rules, slopping as much on the table as went into their bottles. You know guys. However, when it came to the blind tasting, they could distinguish their wines from the others.

As women, we jokingly chided them on, not only the mess they made, but on not following the rules. They did not measure accurately. They exceeded the total volume. Can you believe that one of the guys actually added plain water to his bottle?

Girlfriends, this was definitely something we were not shown to do. The guys were not taking this as seriously as we girls were. They were just playing and having fun.

Yet, at the end of the taste test, the bottles were unwrapped and we found out the guys labeled their wines after us with an affectionate name only we would know. We, girls were both so touched and felt so badly that we did not even think to name our wine after them.

It was their way of giving. They were giving their efforts and their wine to us 100%. It's the little thoughts that make the wine taste sweeter! It is the little things that make life sweeter.

We need to remind ourselves of those special, endearing moments when our guys do special things just for us. It is these little things that demonstrate just how much he treasures us – no matter what, and he knows that we treasure him no matter what.

Professional

Unconditional love does not mean being taken advantage of or taking advantage of someone else.

All relationships have conditions. Yet, if you fail to go into a relationship with the goal of giving 100% you will never get 100% in return.

Think about your parents. Most likely, they gave you a 100% and they expected 100% effort from you. Giving you 100% was conditional upon your behavior and meeting their expectations.

As a parent, you give 100% to your child, although, there are conditions the child needs to meet. These conditions are crucial to developing them into better people. By the conditions we set, they learn important life lessons to enhance their chances for a rich and rewarding life.

At the end of the day, who will be there for you?

For some women, even adult women, it is their parents, for some it is their husband, for some, they have both.

Friends are also very important. As women, we need time with our women friends. Yet, true friends are few in number. Acquaintances compose a much larger group.

As long as you know the difference between the two, you will prosper and grow in your relationships with them. You will also know when to drop them and move on with your life.

Just make sure, when you sever a relationship, you think about it rationally and not emotionally. Remember, you can never go back and make it right.

Sometimes the relationship will be 50/50 sometimes it will 80/20 or 70/30 or 100/0. It will never be the same for all. It is for you, girlfriend, to decide if the ratio is acceptable to you!

Just like when you were a child on the playground teeter-totter, you and your friend found it difficult to ever achieve an even balance. Eventually, it would tip one way or the other. Expect that in relationships.

The scale in chemistry class never balances without a lot of concentration and planning. Diligent concentration in a relationship can help balance the relationship scales. The dynamics of a friendship and a relationship will be rebalanced over the days, weeks, months and years at different ratios.

Unconditional love is an unlimited way of being. We are without any limit to our thoughts and feelings. In life we can create any reality we desire. We just need to choose where to focus our attention.

There are infinite imaginable possibilities, when we allow ourselves freedom to go beyond our perceived limits. If we can dream it, we can build it.

Life, through unconditional love, is a wondrous adventure, which excites the very core of our being and lights our path with delight.

V. Guys are the ultimate recyclers

"Guys are the ultimate recyclers – we recycle everything…" Garth James

Personal

I remember when I was going for an evening out with my husband.

We were driving separately and met at a restaurant. One of his employees was dining at the same place and the employee and I left at the same time.

As the valet pulled up with my black, V12, convertible Jag, he commented, "Isn't that the car, your husband's ex-wife bought him for his birthday?" I said, "Yes it is, and it is a great car".

This was an example of a man's idea of recycling. Frankly, my husband says I look a lot better in it than he does.

Another example was when my husband asked me if I liked cruises. I said I would take a cruise when I was too old to do anything else. I wasn't ready to be regulated to the shuffleboard gang yet.

About a year later, I found two expired cruise tickets in a drawer. He had already paid for the cruise, but one of the tickets had his ex-girlfriend's name on it. He was trying to recycle a vacation. Had I'd known he'd already had them, I would have at least given them to family or friends.

Men will recycle jewelry, cars, houses and trips. They are the ultimate recyclers. In fact, men will even recycle ex-girlfriends.

If the ex-girlfriend was nice, yet for some reason there was just no chemistry between them, he has no problem telling his best friend to ask the girl out. Men consider this recycling.

We, girlfriends, would see it as disloyalty. We would never date our girlfriend's ex-anybody. If we did, we will no longer remain friends, regardless of what happened.

Oh, and about the jewelry thing, we would prefer not to know that the jewelry our husband chose for us is the same jewelry he chose for his exs.

We want to think we are the only one. We want to believe that the special diamond he bought was just for us, not one he got in a divorce settlement.

I learned this lesson in my twenties. I was dating a guy from Boston, while I was living in Dallas.

He bought me this beautiful black pearl ring that was too big for me, he said "he would get it resized and mail it back to me".

Long distance relationships are always difficult. One day, I received the girl's version of the "Dear John" letter in which I was informed that we were breaking up.

The ring was not enclosed with the letter.

Girlfriend, keep the ring. You can resize it later. I am sure the ring is now on the new girl's finger. He "recycled" it.

Lesson learned.

Recycling is what men do and will always do because their attitude is "don't throw away a perfectly good anything". It makes some kind of sense when they put it that way. Yet, girlfriends, we tend to see it as something horribly insensitive and nothing we'd even consider.

We just need to remember our guys are the ultimate recyclers and learn from the realization!

Professional

If you want to keep a girlfriend, you never date anyone they know, used to know, would like to know, or has talked about in the past, present or future tense.

Therefore, girls, it is simple!

No "recycling". No sharing ex-anything.

We like to share stories, yet, never guys. We just do not understand how anyone could do that.

Perhaps, unlike guys, we tend to share intimate details with our girlfriends. We share our dreams, our sex thoughts, our sexual activity, or lack thereof, our past and present history with our current beau, ex-boyfriends or ex-husbands. It is this intimacy with a girlfriend that causes us not to want share, to "recycle".

Guys, on the other hand, do not share intimate details of their lives and relationships with their "buddies". If they share anything about a current or past relationship, it's without any details.

They just say it was "good", it was "bad", "We didn't click", "I scored" or "She was the best", then follow up with the obligatory, "How about those Cowboys?"

That's all they say?

Where's the fun in that?

VI. Virtue

"The world and all things are valuable; but the most valuable thing in the world is a virtuous woman" Muhammad

Personal

I remember how important it was, whether I was dating or married, for a woman to have respect from the one they love. Respect springs from the practice of virtue. Self-restraint is the price virtue demands.

Girlfriends, the concept of virtue is passed down from our mothers. It is what helps us stand apart from less virtuous women. It's one of the reasons the guy picks us and not the other girl. To get respect you must make sure you earn that respect from your guy.

Growing up, I was focused on my studies. I was not allowed to date until I was 16 years old. I was the one who waited until I was 22 years old to have sex. It was important for me to be in love.

I was taught that sex was wrong, until you were married. In my day, this included oral sex or any kind of sex.

 I am sure, looking back today, I may have been considered a "tease". The most I did was clothed, rubbing against a guy. I do believe men want sex or at least oral sex and lots of it. Guys, especially teenage boys, are going to have sex. If you are with them throughout high school, maybe it is OK, or maybe not. It's up to us to decide when the time is right, not peer pressure and certainly not our boyfriends.

It all depends on when we're ready. The guys always are.

Girlfriends, my suggestion is just be sure. As a girl, do not confuse sex, with the anticipation of loyalty and respect from teenage boys, or men for that matter.

Virtue leads to mutual commitment and loyalty.

Girlfriends, admit it, we are affected by every relationship we have with men. We, as women, never forget. For women, sex is emotional. It is about love and being in love. Or at least, having a boyfriend who will kiss you, hold your hand and take you on dates. Most of us need the romance and wooing!

Make sure you decide on how you want to be viewed from an early age. It is important to your self-concept. It determines how you see yourself and how others view you.

Good news. You can change it at any age. Bad news is you have to live with all your past decisions.

We compare our current relationships with our past, present and future relationships. Girlfriends, we never forget the boyfriends we had sex with or even some boyfriends with whom we never had sex.

Sex is part of our self-esteem, our confidence and of who we are and what we want to become as women.

I was probably so afraid of disappointing my parents that being virtuous was the best choice. It was ground into me to be virtuous!

How about you? What value is virtue compared to it's price?

Professional

Virtue is an admirable trait in women. Men prize virtue in women they consider marrying.

From childhood, men and women realize the importance of boys being boys and girls being girls. We learned that boys are bad and we, as girls, are good and sweet. Girlfriends, we know we are the ones who make sure the boys behave!

Our mothers teach virtue! Girlfriends, we need to teach our daughters the importance of virtuous behavior and men will flock to them for love and comfort. This is what men are searching for. It's virtuous women they want, respect, love and honor.

Today, women are confusing equal opportunity and independence as a license to behave any way they want. There is a unique distinction between men and women. Each sex has different responsibilities, innate abilities and drives relating to them.

Girlfriends, thank goodness for that!

We think as women and respond as women. And our men think like men and respond like men. We're just wired differently.

Girls, we can pursue our dream. We choose our paths in life.

Guest what? Our man always thinks we are smarter, cuter and sexier than anyone else. We may not be perfect, but we're perfect for him and he is perfect for us!

Wow, just wow.

The problem today is that some women think, to be accepted in a male dominated society, they have to think and behave like a man. Women determine how men treat them. Mothers teach their daughters how to be women. Fathers teach their sons how to treat women. This is the area that is convoluted with women. Girls, we are confusing the two issues of equal rights and our emotional side and desire to seek virtue in a relationship. The feminist theory fought for equal rights for women. It allows us to pursue any career as a woman. This should not be confused with our desire to seek love and marriage in a monogamous relationship.

Today, mothers may raise their daughters to be strong and, sometimes, stress they do not need a man. Mothers want to be able to have their daughters talk to them about sex. Girlfriend, sex was never mentioned in my house except for one word - NO.

Today, many mothers want to bond with their daughters and want them to share their sexual desires and actions. This may sound like a good idea, yet your daughters do not always want to.

Instead, give her the basics of how women are to behave, and always be open to her if she has any questions. Most everything else they will learn from school, summer camp, Cosmo, or their girlfriends.

Mothers, if you don't already have a subscription to Cosmopolitan, get it. You know your daughter is already reading it. Refer to articles in Cosmo as a basis of a conversation about sex. It could be a starting point, common ground.

As women we need to be demure in our behavior and teach our daughters how to be treated by men. Equal rights does not mean it's permissible to ask a man for a date, to call a man, tell off color jokes, get drunk or use profane language. It's not lady-like.

The balance of men and women; wife and husband; mother and father; son and daughter is broken and confused if we fail to acknowledge our differences as well as our similarities.

Mothers have told their daughters they can do anything a man can do. Girls, I am telling you, and I have learned "I can do anything I want to, if I am passionate about it and make up my mind to do it". So can you!

Mothers wake up! Remember how you earned respect and worked your way to a successful career? You want your daughters to strive for the same.

Well, please make sure you teach your daughter virtue. Men want virtue in a woman. This has been true from the beginning of time and will continue through the generations.

Men fear aggressive, manipulative and domineering women. The difference is very important. By telling your daughters and your girlfriends, they can do anything a man can, you change their chance at success.

Mothers, realize if your teenage girls are talking like a boy, calling boys for dates, pursuing boys and having oral sex and all kinds of sex at very young ages. Often the boys are unable to comprehend what is happening. As they mature, men want smart, successful, caring, virtuous and loving women.

Women don't want wishy-washy, insecure men at the one end of the spectrum or abusive and domineering men at the other. The balance of nature depends on men and women creating a distinct balance in the universe together. Somewhere, somehow it is going astray in our modern society.

Women demean their bodies by using sex to get ahead in business, using sex to manipulate a man and <u>using sex to control the relationship</u>. Sex is a natural allure of loving men and women, yet women believed they won when in actuality they lost all the meaning of sex.

Women need sex <u>with love and romance</u>!

We want to be the only woman in our man's life.

We want a man who loves and adores us. We, as women, control how men treat us. Girlfriends, we can have it all!

VII. If I had a hammer, I wouldn't need a husband

"He that is good with a hammer tends to think everything is a nail" Abraham Maslow

Personal

From my personal experience, always let your man use a hammer and just back away. My husband has exhibited, many times, the importance of a man solving a problem with a hammer.

One example was when my husband and I arrived at our lake house and had forgotten the key.

Choice one: It was about an hour and half return drive to get the key. I even offered to go and get it. It made perfect sense to me.

Choice two: The hammer. My husband ended up getting into the garage and found a hammer. I knew that he was in a "Man with a Hammer" mode and he was going to get into the house. As he hammered the door handle off, I backed away and stayed quiet.

Both choices were effective ways at getting the job done. When your man has that determined look in his eye, just let him use the hammer and worry about the door later.

A close friend and his wife were visiting our same lake house and he forgot the key we had given him. We found out a year later from our neighbor that he broke into the house by getting in through a torn screen and jimmying the window. I'm sure, since, I know his wife; she just stayed quiet and stepped back. She was probably the one he had crawl through the window to unlock the door.

This is a universal man's trait. When faced with any problem it's a man's first response to solve it with a hammer or duct tape. If you ask them to solve a problem, they will.

During our first trip through Tuscany, Italy, my husband and I were in Florence and had shipped our bikes for a week of cycling. Somehow, in the process of shipping, the screw that secured the handlebars to the frame was broken and just spinning around. We had no idea how to fix it.

The first thing in the morning, we decided to carry the bike over to a cycling shop. We stopped at the bike shop and an Italian greeted us at the door. He looked like a professional in his one-piece overalls. Just our luck, he did not speak any English, although he seemed to understand what we wanted, after a lot of hand gesturing. He looked at my bike and came back with a hammer.

I was distraught. This was my new bicycle and he was going to use a hammer on it.

36

My husband held my hand and said, "All men have to try the hammer. Leave it alone". After gently tapping with the hammer, the Italian realized it was not going to work. "Maybe", he said, "we should wait for the bicycle mechanic to arrive". My husband knew enough Italian to understand the guy. He was just the cashier.

Finally, the mechanic arrived and solved the problem in about ten minutes. He didn't use a hammer.

Professional

Men and women have different toolboxes with which to solve problems. Men are used to approaching a solution by taking a direct, simple and easy approach.

Women can also make decisions at a moments notice. Girlfriends, we just have a different approach, although the results are, more often than not, the same.

In a relationship, men apply their normal tact. Unfortunately, it is their emotional equivalent of using a hammer, duct tape or WD40. He is basically clueless without being able to use any of those.

So, girls, listen up. If there are problems in a relationship, remember not to expect your guy to use anything but tools they have been given to contribute to a solution.

You have to let him try even when you know it's not going to work. If he has run through his limited relationship repertoire, he is lost. It is only then that he will be open to considering alternatives.

So, don't expect much more from him in a relationship. If you do, you are giving him far more than credit then he deserves and he will never meet your expectations, little less exceed them.

Girlfriends, we need to use our tools to lead him to a mutually satisfying conclusion.

Fortunately, women have a more complete toolbox for dealing with relationships. It is what we excel at. The judicious use of them will cause less stress and have a positive impact upon ongoing and future relationships. Our use of them will allow mutual love to grow and we'll enjoy spending more time together.

Lastly, maybe more importantly, once we engage our men in a relationship discussion, it can get heated. It can get emotional. Just make sure that you've crafted your approach as best as you can. There are a limited amount of relationship "mulligans". Be careful, when and how you use them.

Girlfriends, we know how to use all the tools in our toolbox and to use them effectively. We can even get our man to pull into a gas station and ask directions without him feeling less "manly". Just in case that doesn't work out, have your phone GPS ready in your purse. Don't pull it out except in the most extreme circumstances! It will hurt his feelings.

Remember, he needs to use his tools first, just as my husband did to get into the lake house. Let him get it out of his system. When that's over, we can really get to work with our relationship toolbox. Girlfriends, we know how to use our tools. Use them wisely!

VIII. Breakthrough

"Don't' cry because it is over, smile because it happened" Dr. Seuss

Personal

I told my husband I loved him first and his response was, "Thank you". I told him I was going to give 100%, whether he did or not.

Guys want points. If you give 100%, eventually, he has to do the same, otherwise, he is not the guy for you.

We stayed at the Mayflower Hotel in Washington, DC for a political event. We decided not to leave the room or attend any conferences. We decided to just keep ordering room service: food, wine, and champagne. We didn't even let housekeeping in. We had a "Do Not Disturb" sign on the door and we meant it!

After four days, suddenly I heard a loud noise. Two uniformed guards broke down the door and were standing over our bed. My husband stood up. He is not body conscious and was fine with getting out of bed naked. I, being demure, pulled the sheet around me. There were two cops, a woman and a man in uniform with hands on their pistols.

Needless to say the woman had a smile on her face as my husband put his hands on his hips and asked, "What do you want?" Maybe, she now knew why we weren't answering the door.

I was speechless. We had six room service carts crowded into the living room of our suite. Was this a crime?

We left that day. My thoughts were, if couples are actually having this much fun on a long weekend, they don't want to be interrupted. Girlfriends, isn't that what we, are looking for? The man enjoys it too!

Oh, by the way, I did say my husband is still the sexiest, hottest man (he's also editing this chapter)! It is about the fun, the excitement, taking a walk on the wild side. The "breakthrough" turned a temporary irritant into a lifelong memory.

Professional

As women, we entice our man. We set the stage. We make the commitment.

When the guy wants to be only with you, you'll know that. By the way, it does have to be about love! Love is the cake! The rest is just the icing. We need and want the icing and the cake too. Otherwise, it's not life's dessert.

Girlfriends, we want to have it all! We can have it all!

Find the right guy. Put yourself out on a limb. Take a chance and see if he responds in kind.

Sometimes, it works. Sometimes, it doesn't. Don't worry about it. Know in your heart that some day it will.

Girlfriends, believe me. Never stop trying! You can't expect to get 100%, if your not willing to give 100%.

 Remember it is all about the points for your man!

Make it easier for him to score!

IX. Men are frogs women are princesses

"All princes start as frogs and all gentlemen as dogs
Just wait till it's plain to see
What we're growing up to be
Cause some frogs will still be frogs
And some dogs will still be dogs
Some boys could become men
Just don't kiss us 'til then"
          Superchick Princes And Frogs Lyrics

Personal

As women, we read the tales of how the princess kisses the frog and it turns in to a prince.

Girlfriends, we realize we have to kiss a lot of frogs, so don't give up.

I have kissed a lot of frogs and a few have turned into princes.

Finally, in dating be willing to kiss frogs. You will find it is eventually worth it. Sometimes you kiss a frog and he does become your prince. He becomes the man of your dreams. He is the man that you love and will do anything to please. He is the prince you are looking for.

You will know that when you meet him. Your toes will tingle, your heart will beat faster and you will want to be with him as much as possible.

It is with him that you will share your dreams, your goals and your desires as a couple. Just remember, he married you because you are his princess and you have to be sure to be like a princess.

That means continuing to dress, act and behave like a princess, who is in love with her prince, the one that swept you off your feet. The one who made sure the glass slipper fit, because he searched throughout the lands to find you, his princess.

Girlfriends, we all know the Cinderella story.

Professional

My advices is continue to go out and kiss the frogs. Give men a chance to be your prince. Although, we can give men a chance, perhaps they will never be our princes. If we are fortunate, we will meet ours. It is necessary to realize, after we find our prince, we make sure the relationship works.

We know it!

Men are taught to provide for his girl. He takes care of money and we the home.

Girls, even if we work, we want him to work and provide for us. Otherwise why bother? You can take care of yourself.

So, let's be honest!

It's the simple things. It's up to you to remember events and making sure the house is comforting and pleasant. Some of you may even be able to cook.

We create the atmosphere of the house. It may be lighting the candles, cleaning the dishes and putting them in the dishwasher. It may be as simple as getting him coffee in the morning or an after dinner drink.

Yet, it is always the woman that makes sure that the house is a home. The home should be a place of comfort and relaxation for both of you. It is the place where we can put up our feet and snuggle together.

He is ours, and we are his!

X. Sex and Chemistry – otherwise he is just a friend

"…if a partner is carefully chosen, the resulting chemical bond between the two will likely be more stable as opposed to selecting a partner at random, If sex is added to the chemistry and enjoyed by both, then stability in the relationship is even more likely to be guaranteed" Martin Dansky

Personal

I know, when I first meet a guy, if there is chemistry or not. Without the basic chemistry, you do not get beyond first base.

I have never experienced a relationship that has developed from friendship into love. Love was always first, I had to be swept off my feet and feel wanted by my man.

It is the continuing process of learning about him; the stories we share and the intimate times together. Once you are in love, the chemistry is enhanced and deepens with time.

Girlfriends, it is the simple things that count. It can be him bringing us a rose for no reason, swimming in the pool, lounging in the bathtub or spa with champagne, having a picnic or taking a walk. Some men think it is about doing the big things, buying jewelry and doing expensive stuff, such as taking us on trips or to a fancy dinner.

Girlfriends, we all like that! We do not want our man to stop impressing us! Yet, after we are in love it is about time together, adventures and the simple things, looking over and seeing his face every morning, knowing he is there during the night, snuggling up next to him and feeling happy and safe.

Sexually, you have the freedom to explore everything you dreamed of with someone, who loves and adores you. Sex and love give you the opportunity to play together, laugh together and have the occasional afternoon delight!

It is important to flirt!

Seven ways to keep the Romance and Chemistry (please find more to add to the list)

-Enjoy doing something special for your man, cook a meal or buy takeout and have wine
 and candles
-Give him cards for no reason. If he travels, hide them in his luggage
-Sushi, candles and sexy lingerie
-Sex in the middle of the afternoon

-Book a hotel and spend a weekend in town together
-Chase each other…kiss, bite, run around like two little kids
-Feel sexy, try on new outfits and flirt with him when he comes home

Professional

Make a list of what you want in a man…and stick to the list!

Girlfriends, beware of constantly picking men you may suspect are losers! Listen to your intuition or gut feelings about the guy. Most likely it is right.

If we are honest, most of us want a man who is at least as smart and successful, if not more so, than we are. We want a decisive man, who plans where to have dinner, what topic we will discuss and takes control. Simply, we want a man's man.

Men have no problem with successful women. We think they do. Really, it is we who choose to be with them more and want to do things for them.

Girlfriends, we are natural born caretakers. We are the ones that pick up the groceries and pick up dry cleaning, do the laundry and then get resentful at our man because we did it all. Guess what, he does not care, if we do it or not. So what? It is about us, not him.

Plan time for yourself and to be with your girlfriends, your man will be just fine and have time for himself and his friends.

Know what you are doing, why and decide to be OK with your decision.

It is up to us to keep the love, excitement and sex in the relationship. We are all responsible for our decisions. All of us can change our decisions and take a new path at any time.

The career woman has a confidence rarely seen in the stay at home wife or mother.

You may have your own success either at your career or at home. Yet, you may have given up your career for a relationship and/or children. If it makes you happy, it's good!

Girlfriends, we are the ones who need to find new and exciting ways to continue the chemistry in the relationship. Why? Because we need it!

There are two indications leading to divorce or separation. The first sign is, when sex stops. The second sign is, even if you have sex, after sex, he is golfing, playing a video game, going to the bars to have a beer with the guys on a regular basis or working extended hours. As he is doing this, you fill your time with shopping, having lunch, or going out for cocktails with your girlfriends.

Red Flag – something is very wrong and both of you will either stay together and live your separate lives or someone will find someone else to give him/her fulfillment.

We are human. We need attention. We need love and we need someone to be there, no matter what happens.

So, just have fun and love the man you are with. It is not necessarily greener on the other side.

XI. How can I meet the right guy?

"When you stop trying to find the right man and start becoming the right woman, the right man will find his way to you"... Cher

Personal

Girlfriends, you never know where you will meet your man. The most important step to take is to make sure you are out where you can meet him. Most likely, you will not meet your man at Pilate's class, a book club, a spiritual meeting, a sewing class or in your home.

Where do men congregate? There's normally a herd of them at a bar (I met my husband at one), or at work (though I do not recommend it). You will never know until you get out there and give yourself the opportunity.

You need to be strong, yet not too strong (the guy likes to take care of you). You need to be needy, yet not too needy (you may scare him away). You need to be sexy and feel sexy (more important than how you look is how you feel about yourself), and yes being thin does help, so no emotional eating.

Most importantly, you need to be yourself, because every guy senses when you are trying too hard, looking too desperate, or acting like you are having fun, when you are not.

Wow! As women, we have to do a lot.

Men are who they are. Don't expect them to change. They are just the package you get. If they are a "guy's guy", which is what we are after, then they woo us. They are who they became over years of their life. They are their work, their upbringing, their family, their marriages, their children, their guy friends, their sports, their habits and their routines.

Professional

As women, we choose to separate our work, our home, our past relationships, our family, our upbringing, our children, our fears, our denials, our friends, or lack thereof, our charities and our life. We are an amalgamation of all the above and should be proud of it. So, yes, be the best woman you can be and you will find the best man for you!

Signs that he is not the right man

- You call him more than he calls you
- You ask him to come over and go out
- He sends no cards, gifts or roses
- His idea of a dating is to text message you at the last moment
- You are doing the pursuing instead of the man; if he is not the pursuer, you are a passing fancy
- If you don't like how he is treating, you need to get out
- Sex is the icing on the cake
- Romance and wooing is what women need to make the sex exciting
- Use your woman's intuition, and do not repeat the same cycles with your man that did not work with your exs
- Make a list of some of the qualities you want in your man

You deserve the "perfect "man for you. You can find him. He's out there!

The reality is that men are pursuers. They always have been and will be. They expect rejection from girls, who do not want to dance with them or turn them down for dates, yet they have the option to stop calling or asking you out at any time.

Women who are aggressive in a relationship may cause confusion for the male species, since men may be unsure how to respond.

Women are competitive with other women for a place in the eyes of a man. Women are emotional and share emotional stories with other women. Men share a beer with other men and are competitive with other men only at work or in sports, where it really counts for them, never in romance.

XII. Being in Love...

"Love knows no limit to its endurance, no end to its trust, no fading of its hope; it can outlast anything. Love still stands when all else has fallen" Dr. Wendy James

Personal

Live the "Fairy Princess" story. I have met the right man, who loves and adores me and gave me a "fairy princess" wedding in Florence, Italy.

He wooed me and still does. I want to please him and make him happy. I want to be the best wife.

He proposed on the beach and then together we planned the most romantic wedding with Italian singers, dancers and flag throwers. The only part that was not cooperating was the weather, since the French were dying of the heat and it was over 100 degrees in Florence with no air conditioning.

Naturally, the airlines lost our luggage, so we were in our hillside villa dressed in our British Airlines t-shirts. At least, I carried my wedding dress. It took two days for our luggage to be delivered right before the wedding.

Girlfriend, being in love is what it is all about!

It means you get to share adventures. Those are the memories, which you keep in your heart, laughing and crying about them years and years later.

That is what makes you look lovingly into your man's eyes and know, that no matter what happens, you have each other.

Wow! Yes, just wow.

When you feel like that, you have the right man. My guy is taken! Now how about you?

When have you felt like you couldn't wait to see your man and would do anything to please him? For me, being with my man has been like a roller coaster ride, exciting, non-stop action through the last ten years.

I have had two wonderful men in my life; first for 16 years, then widowed. Now, remarried for ten years and counting. It just keeps getting better and better!

First, nothing is perfect. My guy is perfect for me and I am perfect for him. That is what defines love, relationship and a marriage. I told my husband "he was perfect for me".

Something happened and we had our first disagreement. Evidently, he only heard the word "perfect". I had to tell him "No, you are not perfect. You are just perfect for me".

It is being the best you can be throughout the relationship. After, an accident and surgery, I knew he would be there to love and care for me and I'd do the same for him.

If you fail, are distressed or fall, he picks you up and helps you get through all the good times and bad times and all the challenges in life that befall us as human beings.

Girlfriends, I would never want to know what was going to happen in my life. I just want to experience every moment of every day.

It is about waking up in the morning and reaching over and touching your guy, seeing him sleeping right next to you, curling up next to him after a wonderful night or morning together.

That is what I am talking about. So now, how about you?

Professional

Girlfriend, listen up; this is different from taking advantage of each other or taking each other for granted. It means that you both respect and honor each other and never purposely hurt one another.

We are all human. We make mistakes. Sometimes, we say the wrong thing and we have regrets.

Be sure to say you are sorry. Never, ever embarrass each other in public. Make sure your disagreements are in private. In private you can have your discussions, express anger and air your misunderstandings.

Almost, 90% of arguments are due to miscommunication. Here we go again. Men and women have differences in perceptions of an incident, a comment or something that happened to set one of the parties off.

Some women may say they continually choose the wrong men, the "bad boys". Yet, women often enable that "bad boy" behavior.

Girlfriend, you determine how men treat you. Women set the rules and the boundaries.

Nice women want nice men, whom will treat them with respect and admiration. Men admit they want and need women. Men want a virtuous woman, the one with morals and values.

Women may struggle with this concept and deny they need men. Additional, many women struggle with the concept of virtue.

Some women feel guilty and afraid. We depend on our guy and end conflict with "I'm sorry". We say, "I'm sorry", so many times, even when we know we have nothing to be sorry about.

Women are strong. Yet, when something happens, the worst thing is if we disappoint our man. He is first over anyone or anything.

This is not a bad thing. It is a caring thing. It is what makes us the nurturer and the ones who look to our husband for strength, decisions and unemotional problem solving. Letting go of this fear of failure is one of the most difficult tasks we face in our lives.

We want to have our guy pay attention to us. Regardless of whether we are thin, fat, cute or average. It boils down to sex appeal.

We are the ones who decide to make the guy notice us. We need to make sure we feel confident in ourselves to wear something sexy. We want the guy to notice us outside of our usual routine day or vocation.

There are some women who stop taking care of themselves. They may gain weight and stop caring about their external appearance. Their husband may be there, but really not "there".

The single girl may be home alone. Oddly, the "put together", thin and gorgeous girl has the same problem. She may fail to keep the spark and her sex appeal.

We want to be wooed. The question is what do you do when you are home with your man?

We set the stage. We determine the results and we keep our guy with us. It is worth every minute of effort to do so.

Girlfriend, the result is bliss at its best with a loving, sexual, caring and wonderful relationship.

XIII. The Fairy Princess and our desire as women

"Fairy Tales: "…gave me what I needed most at a critical time in my life: the image of the creative and complex woman, unique to herself but willing to share those considerable gifts with a man capable of intuiting the wealth of her worth hidden beneath the skin…" Midori Snyder

Personal

I believe in the Cinderella story.

As a child, I would read all the fairy tale books. I would come home from school and do my homework and then spend my time reading in my bedroom.

Fantasy and reading were my way of learning, growing and believing in the goodness of people. I developed a firm belief in life's happy ending.

Life gives us challenges. That is true for all of us. Yet, no one I know would trade his or her place with someone else. The unknown is scary.

As girls, we need to dream, believe in the happy ending and be swept off our feet by a prince. That is what love is. Loving is what it's all about. It makes us emotional, caring and sensitive women.

As women, we are strong and caring at the same time. We need to create that loving relationship which makes us whole.

There are many books written on how to find a man, how to play the game; how to manipulate, keep your distance, never let him know your true self. Make sure he is committed, yet you do not have to commit. This distance gives you a persona that is not your true self. If you follow this dating strategy, a man will not truly love you.

If you hold back, play hard to get, it is a game, not love. The one who knows how to play, wins the game but loses love.

The question is, does this road lead to your happiness?

Girlfriend, I believe you deserve a fairy princess tale ending and you can have it!

Professional

We all want to be the "fairy princess" and believe in the potentiality of the Cinderella story. Cinderella ended up with her prince.

Some say it is just a fairy tale. Others say, that women of today do not need a man and women can take care of themselves.

For women, the dreams of having a man are predicated on the fairytale stories that our prince will love us, defend us and provide for us. Happiness with our prince is what we desire.

Like magic, a charming prince discovers Cinderella. The prince searches the world for his princess who fits the glass slipper. The one who is perfect for him, his Cinderella.

Cinderella is the pretty girl, having no control over her life. Her stepsisters are jealous of her because of her looks.

Today, the pretty woman may think that a man is just after for her look. Sometimes she is uncertain if he realizes and treasures the prettiness contains inside.

Average looking women are often jealous of the beautiful woman, just as Cinderella's stepsisters were jealous of her.

Today, women do the same thing. Often, their first thoughts are that a pretty woman must be a bimbo, empty and just a pretty face. It's a natural defense mechanism, but just turn on the television and look at the number of sexy, pretty and smart women on Fox News.

Men are in awe of a pretty woman. They will rescue her and help her out and, yes, date her. Yet, they also want a smart and successful girl. I find that decent men are very respectful of women for their accomplishments.

Girlfriends, continue to dream of the perfect man to date and, perhaps, marry. Often, we decide that it is better to dream and hold on to the dream of "Mr. Perfect" sweeping us off our feet.

Girlfriend, be with a man who is perfect for you, regardless of his faults. Unlike us men have many.

A woman makes her own magic. It is the magic of her energy, excitement and the joy of life that radiates from her. A man is captivated by it and gives back a hundred fold.

To be in love is to be free from the daily drudgery of life. The mundane activities we perform become less mundane, when we are performing those activities for someone we love and who loves us.

Today, many women want to be in control and usually are. We are the ones organizing for ourselves and our man, schedules, activities and social events.

Let us be honest. As women, we believe in the Cinderella story. We need to be in love. We want to have a man who loves us and we expect him to love us forever.

We, as women, are conflicted by the need for independence and the need to have security. Men, never share in this conflict. Men realize their responsibility is to provide, therefore, they fail to understand our struggle with conflict. They just want their woman to be happy in whatever she decides to do.

Women are taught to seek security. Women can set aside pursuing their own ambitions to become mothers. We are busy with our schedules, the housekeeping, the yard work, the cooking and the raising of children. This is a manifestation of the combination of security issues and "guilt", as we attempt to do it all.

Girlfriends, we need to realize that taking care of others enhances the "Cinderella" dream and is an achievable goal. It is something that can be ours.

Therefore, no excuses! It is up to each of us to define and fulfill our dreams.

XIV. Every Girl Wants to be Special and to be noticed

"Just when the caterpillar thought the world was over it became a butterfly"

Personal

I never saw myself as "pretty".

I was the geeky girl, tall, gawky and very thin. I was very shy in high school and most of my classmates at my 25th reunion were surprised I was talking normally and not in a whisper or at all.

I had my group of friends, who were just as geeky as me. We took pride in being the best students. We were seen, goggles on in chemistry class and skipping study hall to take another advanced course.

The sweater I wore on "boyfriends sweater day" was one borrowed from my brother. I said it was from a guy at another school. I really was going out with a guy from another school. He had long dark curly hair, big brown eyes and always wore jeans and an Army jacket.

At a party, I realized the reason for the Army jacket. He had a gun concealed under it. My eyes must have been as big as saucers, because I had never been with anyone carrying a gun.

He was calm, charming and attempted to put me at ease. Evidently, carrying a gun was related to some past drug deal gone wrong. I just wanted to go home.

Regardless, we did keep in touch for a while. I knew this guy would be trouble and I had my whole future planned to get out of this high school, this town and move far away.

Since I used to date him and was considered a geek at my own school, I spent my prom night at home in my bedroom. No one asked me out.

I might have persuaded the gun toting, bad boy to my prom. I was too embarrassed to have him see me among my classmates and realize no one at high school would pay me the courtesy of even talking to me.

Well, by my senior year I did not care. I was an honor student, who had so many credits, I would leave school at noon for my part-time, secretarial job at the school district. At night, I took classes at the community college.

My goal was to succeed. My academic excellence was my passport to cross borders and roam the wide world.

I would free myself.

Professional

Every girl wants to be special!

Girlfriends, we spent our high school days learning to flirt with guys and compete for dates. We compete to be in the popular group of girls, which gave us that clout and access to the desired dating pool.

We read romance stories and watched shows where the charming prince swept his princess off her feet.

We are programed to be emotional. As a result, we want romance and wooing to feel special. We want to be the only one in our man's life.

Little did we realize that teenage boys had a different motivation than we! Their motivation was about scoring and that meant sex. They may appear to be loyal through high school and will always tell you what you want to hear.

Face it, their prime motivation was to have sex. That was their goal.

Although they may have grown older, men's prime motivation remains the same... SEX.

The smart ones find, by wooing us they get the girl. Fortunately, as the men mature, they find deeper satisfaction in developing a relationship with a woman. They actually want more than just sex. They want to have a woman who is smart, successful, and fun to be with. Men also want a virtuous woman. They depend on us to keep everything pleasant, happy, loving and sexual.

In return, we want to be romanced, loved and feel sexy. Girlfriends, this means no TV, no t-shirts, no boxer shorts, no long robes or fuzzy slippers. Remember the little sexy outfit works.

Some women come home and put on their sweats and take off their makeup. Other women come home and take off their business suit and put on a sexy, little dress and dance in front of the fire and look lovingly into their man's eyes.

Which one are you?

It's up to you to put forth the smallest of efforts.

Women can fall into a routine. All of a sudden life is about working, picking up the laundry, going to the store and taking care of the children.

Girlfriends, it is up to us to maintain the wooing, the love and the romance.

We need to be recognized as special. We take the time to plan a night out on the town, a night at home with candles and a sexy outfit, or a social event with friends, where can dress up and be dazzling.

Put your babysitter on your speed dial for these special occasions.

We've been manipulating men for millennia. Certainly, we have the skills to lead them into situations and actions that bring pleasure to him and, in return, get pleasure from him.

The balance is giving him his own time, while we plan time together to continue and promote the love and adoration we had when we started our relationship.

Share your life with freedom in thoughts, sex, desire and goals with someone who cherishes you.

A man and woman should share their life over the years. It is important to remember to keep and enhance the relationship. Little surprises work!

Make sure your man is first. Maintain what is important in your life. Continues to grow beyond your man through, work, children and/or charity events.

"A woman makes a house a home" is not a hackneyed bromide. It's the truth.

Home for you and the ones you love should be a refuge. It should be a place of comfort and peace, made of love and happiness.

If you are still looking for "Mr. Right", be warned.

There was a study published by Psychological Science. The results found that men's success in dating is based on more promiscuous orientation. This sounds very much like the attraction women have for the "bad boy". We love them.

Men are used to being in the teenage mode to attract the girl. The man learns how to woo us, charm us and make our heart race.

As the study shows he is just after sex.

Really?

We actually needed a psychological study to tell us this?

The upshot of the study is simply this...as women, we need to focus on the types of men that we want to date. Is he is the type of man who will provide us with the relationship we want to have in the long term?

Girlfriends, men still want sex and approach us with a "promiscuous orientation" when dating. That is what boy's and men do – score. We on the other hand control the relationship and how our man treats us!

Girlfriends, we want to be the girl that our man wants to introduce to his mother! It goes back to boys and men are always angling for sex. We want more and eventually, as men mature, we pick the right man for us. It happens. He loves us above anyone else!

XV. Do you wear your sexy underwear for you or your man?

"All cats are grey in the dark" – Benjamin Franklin

Personal

I remember the first gift my husband bought me when we were dating. It was a small blue box. Yes, Tiffany. This was my first blue box with many more to follow. Inside was a gold Tiffany heart. We had only been dating 14 days and he gave the necklace to me at lunch on Valentine's Day. He told me later that he thought I did not like it, because I was just shaking so much I could not put it on. Finally, I asked him to help me with the clasp.

My boss at the time was also a mentor, so I asked him what he thought. Being a guy, he said, "Check to see how many he has stored in the drawer. If he gives every girl the same gold, heart necklace, then you are in trouble. Otherwise, just wait and see".

My husband bought another gift for me. I arrived home and opened a package and it was from Victoria Secret. It was a white, silk gown and white, silk robe. Since that time, he buys me shoes, sexy dresses and outfits about every month.

Guys listen up! It is not about the cost of the gift. It is about the gesture to make you give your girl something special. I remember listening to the news about a husband who gave his wife a rose everyday and put it by her bedside.

That is what I am talking about!

Professional

Girlfriends, we want to feel sexy. Remember, "All cats are grey in the dark". That means the guy does not care how we look. We can have the lights on, off or dimmed. Whatever makes us comfortable and feel sexy works for us and for him. It means you need to enjoy the moment as much as he does and realize he loves you.

So, if you feel a couple of pounds heavy, or look in the mirror and see some wrinkles, realize he does not care. He just wants to be with you!

Men like us naked. Girlfriends, we may think we are putting on the sexy outfits, dancing and singing for him. Yet, we are doing it for us! We need to feel sexy and attractive. He always appreciates the effort. Make sure you have variety in your life with your man, wear a sexy outfit, sing and dance in the kitchen, hop on the kitchen counter or greet him at the door in just a coat.

We do sexy things for us and for our man. We want to be noticed, kissed, chased around the room and treated like the sexy girls we are!

XVI. My Princess Dress

"How can a woman be expected to be happy with a man who insists on treating her as if she were a perfectly normal human being?" - Oscar Wilde

Personal

I am not sure which Christmas Eve is more memorable, but one is when my husband bought me a fairy princess dress, it was fitted, short and with a full chiffon lacy skirt. I immediately went into the bedroom to change, adding white stockings and high heels.

The dress had gold armbands and gold headband accessories. After curling my hair and putting on makeup I came out into the living room and asked, "Honey, what are the batteries for"? He lifted up my chiffon skirt and put the batteries in the concealed pocket and my dress lit up in gold optical fibers.

He turned off the lights and I was just amazed. I ended up in the piano room, alit by my princess dress, as he listened to me play. By the way, my husband bought a baby grand piano for me and had a room built to place it in. It has a black and white marble floor and a skylight to let the sun in by day and the starlight by night.

Oh, you want to know about the second most memorable event for a Christmas Eve? I had just taken a year off to finish my dissertation, my final project, to get my Ph.D. My research topic was "Executive Women Balancing Career, Marriage, and Children".

I had no idea my husband had found my dissertation and taken it to get published. He had a picture of me on the front, written my biography on the back, had it hard bound, made 30 copies and stacked them in boxes around the Christmas tree.

These are some of the special things that husband and wife do for each other. It adds to the memories of loving and being loved!

Professional

Over the years together, husbands and wives sometimes forget to do something special for each other.

Girlfriends, we never want to be treated as "normal"! We want to be treated as special! We want to laugh and giggle and be so surprised at something unplanned and unexpected.

Guys, that means taking us out for dinner and dancing. Buying a rose or flowers and being interested in our new dress or outfit. Just notice it, even if you did not buy it!

Girlfriends, that means make sure you do not forget your man!

Buy him something special. Get him silly cards for no reason. Plan a new activity you know he would like to try and never had.

For my husband, an instrumental rated pilot, it was "Air Combat" flying in a light attack aircraft with a top gun instructor teaching him combat maneuvers. All the memories were caught on video camera, inside the aircraft, while challenging a friend to an aerial combat "dog fight".

Another experience, I arranged for him was to go through a "shoot house", a live fire exercise, where he and five of his friends learned to clear rooms. This was all taught and supervised by a national and international champion in combat pistol competition. Again, this entire event was all caught on video to memorialize the experience!

Girlfriends, the element is to surprise him! Believe me he will appreciate it as much as you do his special gestures for you!

Yes, we have to be accommodating. When he buys you a princess dress or more "naughty" outfits, put them on and have fun!

You can always plan a weekend at a hotel, just for the two of you! Treat yourself to a sexy dress and dine together at a fancy restaurant. Of course, make sure the night of romance extends to room service and champagne!

XVII. And the worst feeling is I do not exist

"I am invisible, simply because people refuse to see me" Ralph Ellison

Personal

I was dating a fabulous guy, seven years younger than me. We had chemistry and he was so attentive and caring. Then it changed. He made me feel invisible.

We had a wonderful night in a great hotel. The next day, when we kissed and walked off the elevator, his boss was in the lobby. He did not introduce me. He did not acknowledge me. He did not say a word to me. I just walked out the door and ended up driving home feeling lost and confused.

We had been dating for quite some time. I had recently, lost my husband. I was new to the dating scene. I just did not understand how a man could make me feel so invisible, like I did not exist. It was one of the worse feelings in my life.

We did see each other after that. For me, something was missing, because he did not have a clue that he did anything wrong.

It made me realize that being invisible is the worst that can happen to a woman in a relationship.

Girlfriends, once you feel you are not recognized, it is over. We want to process and maybe, justify the pattern, the hurt, the relationship and the feelings of being an object.

I wrote a short story about the "Invisible Man Caught in Time", while I was in a café with my husband. It was about a homeless person I saw on the opera square in Bordeaux. A portion of the story is as follows:

"The man stares upon the massive clock in the opera square and the hand clicks into the next five minute mark, he turns and slowly walks, pulling his luggage, to the end of the square to glance at the opposite clock. The man wears a white shirt with a button down green sweater and khaki pants. He is trapped in time between the matching clocks on the square.

People fill the square, as they leave the opera house and evening's dusk descends. French women in five-inch heels, wearing flowing dresses in a rainbow of colors, grasping their lover's arm and laughing as they walk through the square with the clocks.

Over the years, the man "lost in time" walks between the two clocks and fades into the scenery. No one glances his way. He becomes invisible.

As the evening fills the square with laughter, "The Man Caught in Time" is invisible to anyone passing.

If there is so much as a glance at him, it is downcast. He passes the years in a repetitive time warp...homeless, forgotten and lost in time."

My husband, sitting with me at the outdoor café, notices my writing in my traveler's journey. He watches the man's journey back and forth and how the clocks in the square are as poetic as the music from the opera house. He gets up and approaches the "Man Caught in Time" and asks in perfect French "Can I help you"?

The homeless man stops, looks at the stranger and pauses; he takes a moment to speak after so many years of silence. He responds in a low voice, "Bonsoir, oui", yet at this point he is unsure how to respond to the kind man. The "Man Caught in Time" is finally visible again.

After years and years, one man's kindness restores the homeless man to humanity".

Professional

As women, we want to be loved. There is no worse feeling than being with someone who makes you feel invisible. Once, your man makes you feel that you are non-existence or a non-entity, then it is already over.

If you feel like you no longer exist in their world, your man closes you out and ignores you. It means trouble in the relationship.

Men, more than women in general, need some time to watch TV, play videogames or just have quiet time. The reality is that we are emotional. We have a need to explain, reveal our thoughts and communicate our feelings. If our man yells, it is better than if they clam up and treat us as though we do not exist. To be a non-entity causes us to doubt our security.

It is ironic that a smart woman will let a man treat them like that. They have no one to blame but themselves. It is no different than how we treat the poor beggars on the streets. Do we turn our head away and pretend they don't exist?

Do you feel that your man does that to you, when you need to see him or talk to him?

Many men have to have all their "boxes" separate. Their biggest fear is that the boxes could collide and spill over into each other. The man needs to keep all his boxes orderly.

How many of us compartmentalize our life? This is my work box, my family box, my sex box, my love box, my children box, my fun box and, heaven forbid, let's not let the borders blur, collide and crash together.

If one box opens and spills over into another, the fear rises. Can you see the fear in your lover's eyes? You may find that the man is putting his boxes in order. You get attention only when he decides to pull out your box.

How do you deal with it?

When he pulls out "your box" less frequently, you start to feel avoided. One of your responses may be to lash out in anger and hurt. This is when he will walk away and you may never hear from him again. You hope he has learned a lesson, misses you and will come back. Believe me, he doesn't have a clue of what you are angry about or why.

All the beautiful words, the loving words, the special caring words mean nothing without action. It is our actions, especially when taken by surprise, which reveals all about ourselves.

Be aware and moderate your actions and reactions.

We can push away our feelings and thoughts only for a short time. Then, we have to make a decision to cope with our fears and desires, change the dynamics of our relationship or seek out a new relationship.

It is your choice. You can decide, today, how you want to proceed.

Girlfriends, just realize that in making a decision you may choose door 1 or door 2. You can choose another door down the road, yet, realize that those in your life also get to choose and may no longer be part of your life.

We all have choices! Make yours!

XVIII. Active Participation

"Marriage is the highest state of friendship. If happy, it lessens our cares by dividing them, at the same time, it doubles our pleasures by mutual participation" Samuel Richardson

Personal

First it is about love and romance. As women, we want to be loved and adored.

From my experience, a relationship is always about giving 100%, because that is what you want to do. Never think twice about what you will receive. You will get 100% because you gave it.

Girlfriends, it is about love. Love is sharing and caring with no boundaries or guidelines when both of you, respect, care and love each other. We, as women, always know when we have a man who meets those requirements. We know it in our heart. We strive to make it happen.

I have been loved and have loved. I have been dumped and dumped others. I have dated the wrong men, yet never expected more from them than what I received.

The most wonderful time in my life is when I have loved the one who loves me. It is more than special. It is the best you can ever ask for. It makes all the "ups and downs", "trials and tribulations" of life worth every moment.

I am the girl who believes in the "knight in shining armor". I believe in the Cinderella story. I believe in a fairy Godmother. I believe in the romance composed of wooing, flowers, dancing, diamonds and sexy clothes. I believe in my man and always will, because to do less is to accept less. I believe I deserve the best.

Girlfriends, "How about you? Do you feel as though you deserve the best?"

Professional

Relationships are about active participation. Both parties have to be active in the process of caring, doing, loving and mutual participation to make it work.

Women need to realize there is a difference between total reliance and total dependence. A man wants a woman to rely on him. He wants to rely on her. Dependence leads to the fear of potential loss, the fear he will leave, the fear that you have no other choice than to be with him.

What will you do if he walks out the door? These self-defeating thoughts often lead to the result you feared for so long. Fearful thoughts lead to certain behaviors.

Girlfriend, we need to rely on a person in a relationship, yet, you cannot be totally dependent on them. Total dependence will lead to destruction. Total reliance upon yourself does not allow you to open up your heart to love.

You are responsible for your actions and how you respond to circumstances you can't control. It is painful for women to admit that there is, or was, a "cause and effect" in the relationship.

You can be the victim, or you can accept responsibility. You learn and grow from the experience or not. It is easier to be the victim and blame others for your fate, than it is to take responsibility and admit we changed or destroyed our relationship all on our own.

Girlfriends, take responsibility. We are not victims!

XIX. Mirror, mirror on the wall, who is the fairest of them all?

"Have no fear of perfection you will never reach it" Salvador Dali

Personal

As girls we, always remember the story of a Queen, who animates a mirror, while reciting, "Mirror, mirror on the wall who is the fairest of them all"? The queen is jealous of Snow White, her stepdaughter, and attempts to kill her many times. Snow White eventually becomes a Queen with beauty and poise.

I remember a poem about a butterfly. It states, if he is meant to be yours he will stay. Otherwise, let him go to fly away.

The only good thing about the poem is I ended up applying its wisdom to my relationships.

If I did not think my guy wanted to be with me, I figured I should not want to be with him. The only problem is, sometimes, the guy did want to be with me and I misunderstood and for some reason assumed he did not want to be with me, so I disappeared.

Poof, I was gone. Sometimes, that is good. Sometimes it was because I had not matured enough to realize that for him, my guy, I was the fairest of them all.

Since that time, I have grown. I know I have the stubborn gene in me that I need to recognize and cope with.

Oh, that is right! I am a trained psychologist and should be aware of my relationships.

As my mother always said, "Easier said than done".

It seems we can always tell someone else what to do. Yet, we can rarely take our mother's advice.

Professional

As women, we can be on our own. Sometimes, we will leave a relationship before we even give it a chance. Then there are the times where we give the relationship an underserved chance.

Wow, we have to take the time and reflect upon the relationship. We need to rely upon our gut feelings to guide us. Is this guy right for us? Most women I know today are smart and can figure it out all on their own. They can run a multi-million dollar company, yet need to be the fairest girl of them all for their guy.

There is no reason that women cannot have it all, do it all and accomplish it all.

Women are the ones who put the pressure on themselves to succeed in marriage, as a mother, and pursuing a career. I find that the women I meet, who are successful, have managed to overcome great obstacles to continue that successful behavior and apply it to their home, marriage, children and giving back to the community. We all want to be the fairest of them all like Snow White.

I believe in fairy tales. I believe fairy tales can come true.

What about you?

XX. What do you want to talk about?

"The quality of your life is the quality of your relationship" Anthony Robbins

Personal

I remember feeling neglected by my husband. We were in the same room together, but watching television shows. It used to be we liked to snuggle together.

Now, I realize, I resented TV time! I asked him, "Why can't you spend the same time talking to me as you do watching TV?"

Being a caring husband, he turned off the television, looked at me and asked, "What do you want to talk about"? I could not think of anything to say.

Now, I was caught in a situation where I realized I just wanted attention. I did not know what we would talk about. I realized it was my fault. I had no idea how to change situation. I am not sure what I wanted, in the way of attention. I finally decided I wanted an activity a day with him.

I find that men are easy. Girlfriends, we make it difficult by getting all our emotions and our need for attention involved in many situations.

Girlfriends, we need to be sure we have a plan. I know I am the one who plans our social activities. When we do not have a social event, I have no one else to blame but myself.

I know sometimes I just need time with my husband. I need time alone with him. We both enjoy doing an activity, golfing, bicycling, scuba diving or sharing a romantic dinner together. It works for both of us.

Girlfriends, we have to schedule it and let him know how much we treasure our time together.

Professional

Girlfriends, we realize what we are doing and what we want in a relationship. As women, do we make the situation the best it can be?

Men will always find other men to hang with. Boys will be boys.

We have to develop the same sharing and caring experiences with our women friends.

Girlfriends, we have a need to share a story, an experience or an event. I think we need to do the same with our men.

They can go out anytime and have a beer with the guys. If he is a guy's-guy, then it works just fine for him.

The same thing happens in couple's relationships. More women tell me that, if their husband does not like the other husband or date accompanying a girlfriend, he tells you afterwards to go out with your girlfriend alone in the future.

One of my girlfriends, with whom I was attempting to get together, said, "If my husband does not like yours he might walk out". I said, maybe, my husband might walk out first. Fortunately, many years later, we all remain good friends.

The dynamics of men and women will always be different. That's what makes it work!

I remember that, after traveling for a week, I came home and my husband was in his robe, unshaven and had not showered for a while. He never left the house. He said he found out about "dining in". They would just show up and deliver food. He found no reason without me there to get out of his robe, shower or shave.

The point is men need women to keep them normal. Otherwise, they spend their lives on the couch, watching TV, ordering out for food and drinking beer.

We need our man to notice us! We are needy in this way and we know it.

We make the decision of how we want the relationship to evolve and to expand our horizons.

Girlfriends, next time you want to talk to your man, make sure you have a subject to discuss.

By the way, a "discussion" does not mean bringing up a gripe from six months ago. It needs to be an intellectual or informational topic!

XXI. Overcoming yourself

"One who gains strength by overcoming obstacles possesses the only strength which can overcome adversity" Albert Schweitzer

Personal

As women, we sometimes doubt the person inside. We may perceive ourselves as a young girl and filter our perceptions based on our childhood encounters.

I was born in the generation where women were supposed to stay home and have children. I was able to get a scholarship to college and was a top honors student. My motivation was to have a career.

I was afraid of relationships. I was insecure. I never felt pretty. I never dated in high school and considered myself an ugly duckling.

It is a perception. We can decide to change it, if we desire to do so.

My self-perception helped me focus on my studies and not boys.

Girlfriends, we have doubts and learn behavior by watching our mothers, female mentors and our friends.

Sometimes, these are great experiences and sometime leads to us to be concerned, confused and filled with self-doubt. Only when we become our own unique individual and realize our characteristics, charm and confidence, do we begin the process of overcoming the doubts we have about ourselves.

Professional

Girlfriends, overcoming yourself is to recognize these signs, to acknowledge them and reflect on who we are and what we are doing, or not doing.

What is important is not appearance, but the real person inside.

Psychologically, positive thoughts can be brought to the surface. These thoughts confirm that you are a good person, a caring friend, mother and wife.

Often doubts reemerge. We may consider ourselves to be unworthy and think, "Shame on me, for believing I can do it all. I can be happy without the support and love of my friends, family, and children". We need to clear our minds of those doubts and feel as though we are deserving of all those blessings.

We, as women, have so many options, so many choices and we can accomplish what was impossible just a generation ago. We can do it all. We can choose our roles in life.

If we start to have doubts about ourselves, then it may adversely affect our relationship with our guy. It can bring emotions to surface that are incomprehensible to him. A woman creates an image of herself, and accompanying behavior that affects her husband or boyfriend.

Women can push a man away by our fears, insecurities and failure to believe he loves us for who we are inside as well as our outward appearance. Once a woman starts having doubts about her self, it will affect her marriage.

Women, if we are confused about ourselves, we are left with the process of first overcoming ourselves. Sometimes, "the stay at home mom" may feel as though she does not contribute to the household. Girlfriends, we can feel less important and more dependent on a man. Often, the stay at home mom believes her worth is not as great as the working mom. This is not true, nothing is more important then raising children. We can choose our own path to happiness.

Girlfriends, whether working or not, we take on the tasks of buying the groceries, doing the laundry, the cleaning, taking the children to their events, cooking and then may resent our man because we are doing it all.

Guess what? He does not care. He just wants us to be happy. What will really happen if the clothes are not washed or you have to order dinner in?

Working, or not, is a choice we make. Our man does not care, but we do. Then we may search our souls as to what our purpose is. At some point, the children will grow up and have their own lives. They should. That is how we should be raising them.

As a psychologist, I counsel women to have something that's theirs alone. Pursue your career, hobby or charity work and <u>accomplish something that is yours</u>. We get the career, the lover or husband, the children and even the dog, yet feel something is missing. How can that be? Is it about us, or our relationship? Girlfriends, only you know the answer.

We have every opportunity to attempt to please. Generally, we are pleasers. We want to be liked, be successful and happy. We want others to see the image that is reflected in the mirror, a woman who is confident, successful and in control.

Is it about our evolution and the struggles over the generations to change what women can and cannot do?

Alone is better than being in a bad marriage. <u>However, alone is lonely</u>. You may have your friends, yet they are not there day in and day out, when you are struggle with issues. They are not there the moment you call or fling open the door to share you glorious day or the "trials and tribulations" of your life.

Girlfriend, it is about sharing all this with your lover or your spouse, who is there through all your ups and downs and moments of confusion. At the end of the day, you know he is yours!

XXII. Do you have a dog or a cat and are you single?

"There is no psychiatrist in the world like a puppy licking your face" – Bern Williams

Personal

I had two Persian cats. After I met my husband, I had to find them a new home because he is very allergic.

I have friends who are single and they have dogs and/or cats. If you spend more time with your pet than your man, there is a problem.

My husband and I now have a blonde lab and she is the best. Girlfriend, it is always necessary to remember the dog or cat does not replace a relationship with a man.

Pets can take away from dating opportunities. You may have to leave earlier than intended to feed, water and give them attention. You may decide to stay home, because you have a wonderful pet to snuggle up with. A spur of the moment long weekend trip? Forget it. You've got to board your pet.

Pets are wonderful; they do not talk back, always attempt to please, give you that sad look and wags its tail. A dog will listen to you, cock its head and make you feel that all is good.

Listening and sharing is important; we all need someone to share our thoughts with. Pets listen with no judgment. They look like they're really interested in what you're saying and sit at your feet.

Professional

Girlfriends, the reality is you have to be out and about with people to meet someone. You can live your life with your pet, or you can choose to find your man and then have a pet. Just always remember a pet is a pet and human relationships are first.

No, I am not attempting to upset pet owners or any organization that helps pets. It just means that you can have both your man and your pets. Just make sure that your man is first

I bought my two cats for my late husband, because he liked cats. They ended up being my cats.

I bought our blonde lab puppy for my husband and she is equal opportunity pack dog. She knows my husband is the alpha, but I am the one who takes care of her.

Of course, I am attached to pets. Women are the nurturers. The men want their dog to be at their feet and wag their tail and sometimes fetch. Men tend not to be into the maintenance of them.

Girlfriends, we assume the responsibility of making sure the dog is fed, walked, watered and their basic needs met. We become emotionally attached with our pet.

Just make sure in the process you take care of your needs and focus on your man!

XXIII. Worry, worry, worry

"There is only one way to happiness and that is to cease worrying about things which are beyond the power of our will" Epictetus quote

Personal

Worry, worry, and worry! Is it worry, or motivation? There is a fine line between the two.

Girlfriends, do you worry? If so, what is it about?

I worried about so much. Maybe it is just a family trait. I worried about getting into college. I worried about getting a job. I worried about my career and moving up the ladder. I worried about time frame of completing my Ph.D. and I worried about my dissertation. Yet, interestingly enough, I pushed myself to be better and more successful.

Amazingly, despite the worry I was successful.

I worry that I would not live up to my expectations. My expectations are higher for myself than anyone expected of me.

I find many women are the same. Their expectations are higher than anyone expected of them. They aspired to be the best they could be and continued to study, research and work at learning.

Professional

As a psychologist, worry may lead to unhealthy obsession. Motivation and hard work lead to success!

Girlfriends, it is much easier to analyze our past actions. As is said "it is easy to be an armchair quarterback the next day".

Work and motivation are necessary in everything we pursue in our life!

Yes, it even applies to relationships. Do you worry and obsess about building a relationship? Sometimes, worrying about the relationship leads to mistrust or obsession, both negative emotions.

Girlfriend, there's a simple checklist to see if you are obsessing over a man

-Do you pick up the phone and start to dial his number?
-Do your drive by his house?
-Do you attempt to go places you know he frequents with the chance you will run into him?
-Do you spend time a great portion of your day thinking about him?
-Do you continue to check his Facebook site?

-Do you believe that the relationship is something it is not?
-Does your fantasy transform the man into something he is not, but who you want him to become?

If you answered yes, to some or all the questions, you need to realize you could be becoming obsessed.

He may not be the ideal fantasy man you have constructed in your mind. You are setting him up for failure in your relationship. He may never reach your "ideal".

As far as men are concerned, I did obsess when was dating. I continually asked myself, "Will he call? Why didn't he call? Should I call?" Yet, I learned to do a couple of things, if I did not hear from him, I deleted his phone number from my cell phone and computer. That way, after a couple of glasses of wine and feeling lonely, I was not tempted to call him.

Girlfriend, stop and move on!

As a result, I spent many Saturday nights home alone and learned to enjoy my own company. This may have been beneficial to my career, since I spent the time studying and writing instead of dating.

Girlfriends, we need to be comfortable in our own skins. Then, when we meet our man, we just get a wonderful guy, who complements us and helps us to be better and grow!

I know my husband challenged me to pursue my dreams. He is the first I go to for advice and guidance! He is always honest and has my best interest at heart, because he loves me!

Girlfriends, we know the guy needs to do the pursuing and wooing! I was raised to make sure the boys wooed me, called me and asked me out for a date.

We worry about our looks, age, weight, health, work, friends, our men and our children. Wow, we just worry a lot! Healthy women know when they are worrying and know how to keep it under control. If our worry keeps us up at night, it is a burdensome, uncontrollable obsession.

If it continues to happen frequently, it may lead to unhealthy obsession. We need to let it go! Anything that occupies most of our thoughts and adversely affects our life and happiness is unhealthy. We lose control when we let something obsess our thoughts. This creates an emotional imbalance. At this point, we need to know we should stop and seek advice from our healthy friends, or a mental health professional.

Girlfriends, we never forget an adverse incident that happens to us. Unfortunately, we will return to it and rehash again and again. Of course, we know not to do it.

Men assume a past incident is done, over and forget it. I've always wondered how men can always remember baseball statistics, yet, forget an anniversary or a birthday. Of course, this has changed today, because all they have to do it put it on their computer to remind them.

As Toby Keith's lyric goes, "It's not the one you can live with it's the one you can't live without". Find the man that you know you want to be with and who wants to be with you!

We know how to choose our man. We know when we are choosing the "bad boy". That is fine for a short period of time, yet the "bad boys" are not who we want in a long-term relationship.

If you are happy, it is because he makes you happy. If he is happy, it is because you make him happy.

Yes, that is what I am talking about! Caring, loving and being with the one who loves you.

XXIV. Women do not want to be rescued even though they want to be the Fairy Princess

"I wanted to see him as the white knight and was crushed whenever anything normal happened. I wanted to be the princess. Now I'm much more willing to see myself as human and flawed and accept someone." - Jennifer Garner, actress

Personal

The first difficulty, I have is when I hear the word "rescue".

I know I want to be with a man, the man of my dreams, who sweeps me off my feet.

Girlfriends, today, we often struggle with the need to be independent and at the same time feel the desire to be taken care of by a man.

For the man, it is confusing.

We may give conflicting signals. First, "I want you to take care of me". Second, "I can take care of myself".

I want him to be strong, yet not too controlling. I want him to love me. Yet, I want to have my own independence, career and purpose in life.

Girlfriend, even I am confused by my need for both independence and being rescued. I can imagine how my husband gets confused over the mixed messages.

My mother taught me "survival". She taught both my sister and me how to survive. The solution was, "Never have to depend on a man. Always be prepared to take care of yourself". NO!

My mom was strong and a survivor herself. She filled the role of the traditional homemaker, staying at home, raising the children, cooking the meals, getting involved with PTA's, Scouts and being there whenever we needed mom.

I have found survival is not enough. I want to evolve and be the best at what I choose. If I am told, I can't do something, the stubbornness pushes me to overcome what I was told I couldn't do.

Girlfriends, as women we are emotional in personal relationships, yet rarely show it at work.

I remember a quote from an Executive whom I interviewed during my dissertation "*Perspectives of Executive Women; Balancing Career, Marriage and Children*". She said, when she was upset at work, she would go in her office, close the door, lean over and let the tears drop on the desk, so the tears would not ruin her mascara.

Professional

Girlfriends, we are the ones that insure that the family and the relationship are secure. <u>Women are the glue that holds the family together.</u> !!

Over the years, we tend to be the ones who exhibit feminine traits of emotional and sensitive behavior. Men have masculine traits that represent dominance, strength and logic. In the workplace, women have learned to rein in our feminine traits and exhibit the logical thinking and leadership.

We can plan our life and balance it so long as we are aware of what we are doing and why.

Are you a career woman?   Are you giving as much to your relationship as you give to work?
Are you investing as much time, effort and sweat?

By giving, you will get someone who loves you, touches, holds, kisses and makes love with you! It makes the day something to look forward to and, arriving home, having someone to share it with.

Girlfriends, we struggle with wanting to be rescued and taking care of ourselves. The dichotomy is that, when it happens, we want to be independent and taken care of.

We are missing something important in our life without a man. This has not changed throughout the years, generations and centuries.

Therefore, as women, we struggle with wanting to be a princess but not wanting to be rescued.

<u>Girlfriends, let your man rescue you. Both of you will be happy</u>!

XXV. Keep the fire ignited

"I'm very determined and stubborn. There's a desire in me that makes me want to do more and more, and to do it right. Each one of us has a fire in our heart for something. It's our goal in life to find it and to keep it lit" Mary Lou Retton

Personal

Mary Lou Rettons' quote is as true about career and sports, as it is for relationship. In a relationship, it is up to you to keep the fire lit, because, if you do, then you are happy and get what you want.

I am stubborn and determined. Sometimes, that gets in the way of being rational in the relationship.

Girlfriend what do you want?

Knowing about yourself is the first step to making sure your relationship continues to grow and the fire is always lit.

Relationships change.

When I was widowed and started dating again, I would go out with my single girlfriends and watch the interaction between men and women.

There is excitement in the chase, being pursued and dating again. Is the chemistry there? After a certain amount of time, the excitement of a new relationship modifies. When you meet the right man, then the love and chemistry continues to flow and mature.

Over the years, you may get too comfortable. As women, we want romance and we set the environment with our man, to keep it fresh.

Girlfriends, it is up to us to be sexy, flirt and continue to make it exciting in love, chemistry and, of course, sex.

Professional

As long as the fire has some heat, some light and some flame, the fire can reignite the love. If the fire is completely extinguished, it is over and may never be rekindled. When the fire is extinguished he may do the disappearing act. Poof, he vanishes from your life. You are resentful and miserable. You may believe for a time will you never give so much of your life and love to anyone again.

So, in the next relationship, perhaps, the new man in your life loves and adores you, but there is no love and adoration from you in return. This is doomed to fail because you are doing to him what was done to you. How can this relationship have a chance?

Some of you are willing to sacrifice. You may determine that you don't need true love and you settle for less.

After choosing to settle, you may be the one messing up the relationship. Your behavior is no better than the behavior you hated in the past loves of your life.

In a relationship, you may be able to handle yelling, abuse and anger, but not if your man vanishes, walks out or, worse, just ignores you. Yet, did you play a part in causing that to happen?

Once either partner makes the other feel less than significant, the relationship is over!

We, as women, may justify a failing the relationship. "He was a playboy". "He was horrible". "He was the cause of my problems". "He treated me badly". The more you do this, the more you are attempting to make him insignificant to you. It hurts less that way.

Girlfriend, he is significant or you wouldn't discuss him at all. You would just go on with your life and have no more thoughts of him.

Either way, your thoughts need to be "I hope he has a great life and he was a great guy", even if you feel betrayed. You may feel as if he has taken your heart out and crushed it. Perhaps, you are the one who is guilty, because you were unable to love in a mature and giving way.

Girlfriends, I have seen many married couples stay together when the spark and excitement has dimmed. Some of these couples have not had sex (with each other) in months or years. They remain together because it is convenient, or it's for the children, or for the status, or because it is easier than moving on.

We, as women, may be more content with the known than with the unknown. The trouble with the known is if it is not right for us. We may never change and grow and allow ourselves to be open to new challenges and opportunities of a relationship change.

Just think what you might be missing?

The man may stay around, until the woman starts nagging, complaining, never having sex with him and/or he meets someone else. Maybe, he is just sick and tired of the monotony of it all.

What can drive a woman crazy is when her man just leaves one day with no warning, no discussion, no going to a marriage counselor. The woman is angry and shocked because, even though she knows their marriage is no longer one of "being in love", she believes he still loves her. How could someone just disappear?

When the relationship is at an end, move on or your man will.

He may not leave. Instead, he will give his attention to the children, his work and his guy friends. He closes the door of his love on you. Do not be surprised if he walks in one day and out of the blue, says, "It is over". You will be angry and shocked. Your love may then translate into hate and revenge.

The reverse can happen. If you feel he does not give you attention and love. You may decide to have an affair. The new guy promises to love and will marry you when you are divorced.

Then you get divorced and he freaks out and tells you, he is not ready for a serious relationship. He did not think you would actually get divorced. He may be single. He may be divorced and have his own children to take care of. For him it was about safety. It was about sex with no attachments. It may be that he does care for you, yet, he did not expect you to divorce and was not prepared for that.

Girlfriend, if you want to save your marriage do it now before the bond, the fire between the two of you, is extinguished. Yikes!

Women are instrumental in keeping the relationship exciting and making sure the man puts away his other boxes and concentrates on her.

Some of you will decide you can take care of yourself and you are better off being alone. It is very easy to get into a routine of living alone, or with a roommate, instead of a lover.

Your girlfriend will be there for you until she meets a man. Then, the man, not you, will become her priority. You've probably seen your girlfriends fall in love, give all their attention and time to their man and slowly distance themselves from you. Why?

Her first priority is to her man. You feel and see a difference. So you deflect by convincing yourself that you don't want to become like your friend. She can't and doesn't do anything without her man.

Are you happy?

Do you make your guy happy?

Can the fire be relit? Is there an ember that can be fanned into a flame? Is it too late?

XXVI. Communication or lack of Communication in a Relationship

"Men are motivated and empowered when they feel needed. Women are motivated and empowered when they feel cherished" – John Gray

"Once we grasp the two characteristic approaches, we stand a better chance of preventing disagreements from spiraling out of control" – Dr. Wendy James

Personal

Here I am, a psychologist, married for ten years and I still miscommunicate with my husband. Perfect example, I want to have my time to write, so my husband schedules to be busy on other activities and meetings.

Then, I feel neglected and that he is not spending time with me. I get emotional with him. I tell him he has been out every night. He says, "Where do you want to go? What do you want to do? I can cancel and be with you".

Girlfriends, this is when we just need to communicate. Let our man know what we want and when. That does not mean, either one of us canceling previous engagements. It just means letting each other know when you need time together!

A friend of mine indicated he and his wife were going to counseling and he was attempting to empathize. She was upset and, needless to say, he didn't know why and after all it was a week ago. She was being emotional and attempting to convey her needs in the relationship.

The husband decided to write everything down and make sure he had it right so he could talk about it at another time. He did not say a word, just was writing down what she said. Finally, she looked at him and shouted, "Why are you not looking or paying attention to me. What are you doing?" She asked, "Is this for the counselor?" Then she gave him the finger and said write that down". This is not a conversation.

Later the next day, he realized as he was still writing. He ended with the biggest middle finger he could draw. He realized he was angry with her and she was angry with him. He did not know how to address it or change it.

So, like a guy, he just went back to work hoping it would change with time, thinking his wife is just going through a phase.

Professional

Here I have been talking and focusing on love, romance, how to get your man and now this chapter. You must find a way to communicate with your man so he understands you, or it will not work.

Chemistry, romance and sex are all important. Yet, if you do not communicate it may cast a shadow on your relationship.

Girlfriends, lack of communication, failure to talk may cause the relationship to be less than what it could be.

So here we go, women want to be emotional and talk about everything and expect the guy to respond, not understanding he may choose not to talk about it at all. Then, we get emotional and fail to communicate in a way he understands. If we don't then we are just venting.

There is no easy answer for communication, because we just try to relate and do what we do as women. Men do not want long conversations about relationships or communication. They just fail to understand that there are times we just want them to listen. They just want to fix it.

Regardless, the lack of communication will result in our and their unhappiness.

So what is the answer? Being aware of the need to communicate is the first step. Often we see communication through our eyes and lack the ability to see how we are communicating to our husband.

He just sees communication differently and may not understand "just listening". His first inclination is for you to layout your problem so he can find a solution and fix it.

Girlfriends, we need to focus on what we say and how we say it. Men and women are just wired differently and that is a good thing! We, as women, need to realize that our man has a different perspective on communication. He may hear something completely different than what we thought we said. It's how we are communicating. Then we may get angry and feel like he just doesn't want to understand us and is being selfish.

We spend time and work in a relationship. Both sexes learn to accept each other and realize that they may communicate differently. We can learn the difference and grow together in our love.

All relationships are based on expectations. The idea that the man will love you "unconditionally" is just not true. If you search your heart you will know you have conditions for your man. The conditions are love, chemistry, sex and communication!

XXVII. We all want Respect!

"In the end we are separate; our stories, no matter how similar, come to a fork and diverge. We are drawn to each other because of our similarities, but it is our differences we must learn to respect"...Dr. Wendy James

Personal

When I had been dating my husband for a couple of months, we took our first trip to Washington D.C. I told him "I love him" first he said he thought it first.

I told him I would give 100% in the relationship.

Girlfriends, guess what? If you are willing to give 100%, he will do the same.

 I told my husband, since we are getting serious, there is one more request. I said, "I want you to outlive me".

Being the typical man he said, "I can do that! Anything else?" I said, "No, that is it". Of course, I know it is in Gods' hands, since I am seven years younger and we are both healthy. So we started exercising more, eating healthy and having regular check-ups.

Our doctor was giving us our vitamins, based on our blood work. My husband told our doctor, "If Wendy looks like she is going to outlive me, just delete some of her vitamins".

Along with love is respect for one another. That means you keep your disagreements private and never air them in public.

To respect and honor is part of your mutual marriage vows, and his, too.

Professional

Girlfriends, we want respect from our man and want him to be with us. This goes both ways. That means no snarky comments, no demeaning looks or comments behind each other's backs. You may not notice it. Believe me, your friend's do!

There are two kinds of women. First, there are those who manipulate men and play the game. You may feel as though you cannot let him know all about you, or the mystery is lost and he will leave. These women are the ones who use sex to get love and affection, or withhold sex to have a measure of control.

The second kind of women, are the ones who fall in love and loves her man completely. She gives all. To do less is outside of her nature. She loves to be with her man. Loves sex with him. Respects him as much as he respects her!

Girlfriend, which one is you?

If you are the first type, you may become insecure in the relationship, because you assume it will not work, if you do not manipulate him. This may lead to attacking your man, shutting him out of your life or leading your own life and he, his. Is this really a marriage or relationship?

The man looks to a woman for compassion, love, and pleasure with whom to spend his life.

Most men love being married and love their wife. Once the attacks start, the man will run away and find someone else as soon as possible. He will obtain what he wants and needs. It will not be you.

This may cause the wife to be completely surprised when he leaves. This may result, her being angry and desire revenge.

Men and women are users of the opposite sex, if they choose to be. It's a choice!

Girlfriend, you need to choose a man who is right for you. One who you love and adore and who loves and adores you.

So simple! Yet we, as women, sometimes make it so difficult.

Respect and love each other!

XXVIII. Take an adventure

"The word 'romance,' according to the dictionary, means excitement, adventure, and something extremely real. Romance should last a lifetime" Billy Graham

Personal

What could be better than having an adventure with your lover?

My husband wooed me with a bicycling trip in Tuscany, Italy.

He had planned to take me to Italy and see the sites across the country in a limo. I said, "Why would we want to be in a car when we can bicycle, walk or something?" No, I was not a cyclist, unless you count what you do as a kid to get around the neighborhood.

I remember getting a call from him while I was in Las Vegas at the National Broadcasters Association. He asked me what my inseam was, I said, "Honey, girls' don't buy their pants by inseam". He said go to a men's store and they will be happy to measure you for your inseam. I did and found out it was because he was buying both of us bicycles to tour through Tuscany and wanted the frame to fit properly. He gave me a book on Florence and Tuscany for my birthday and signed it "Romantic Italy with you, what could be better". The trip to Tuscany was amazing.

All I know is every time we cycled to a new destination we were looking down on a beautiful view, of where we started that morning. This may be why all places were called Monte such as Montepulciano, Montalcino. Girlfriends, yes, they are the best places for Italian wine after the bicycling.

 I found out, bicycling as a child was nothing compared to cycling through Tuscany! It was scary, when going down the hill, descending so slowly I could have easily tipped the bike over.   My husband said, "Make sure to be careful. Don't fall". Embarrassingly, we have it on tape and believe me; my fear of falling down the hill was so bad that you could hear the brakes squeaking loudly, Eek…Eek. Regardless, we spent two wonderful weeks bicycling in Italy.

What an adventure! You know that your husband loves you when you are sweaty, no makeup on and having to pee in the vineyards. Of course no one was around, until I tried to find a place to pee, then a truck just happens to arrive on the scene.

Girlfriend, play together and you stay together. Have adventures to share. These adventures make great stories throughout your lifetime.

Professional

The question is, are you and your husband playing together? What activities do you share?
How often do you laugh?

Take time to have an activity! So often, we get into a routine that puts us in a repetitive rut.

Girlfriends, if we fail to suggest adventures, where we can get closer together, it may affect the relationship.

Slowly, days may become a repetitive routine of the house, the kids and other everyday activities. Girlfriends, sometimes our husbands think watching TV is together time. We know it is not, we want them to take us out. Even worse is pursuing our interests in separate rooms and believing it is healthy for the relationship. It is not!

If the activity is calming and individually satisfying, it may be good. You have each other, the children and your careers or interests. It is important to make time to look at each other, lovingly, and share special moments.

The simple things are important. How often do you share your day? Talk about events and plan adventures? Or, is it always about the house, the yard, or never talking at all? Maybe you need to have an afternoon delight. Take the time to pursue your fantasies and find adventures you can share with your husband.

Girlfriend that means you need to initiate it! Yes, sex! He is your husband and lover. As a psychologist, I have heard many women use sex as a way to manipulate their man, withholding sex or using sex as a control mechanism. My suggestion is stop! Make sex and adventures something you enjoy together. You did at one time.

It means trying an activity he enjoys doing. See if you like it, if nothing else, he will appreciate the effort!

It is the adventures and the shared experiences that continue to add to your relationship! Just learn to enjoy the roller coaster of a relationship, the ups and downs, the good times and bad. At the end of the day you know you are with the person you love and want to continue to love and with whom to share adventures!

XXIX. Blame it on the Venezuelans: It is their fault

"I praise loudly, I blame softly" - Catherine the Great

Personal

I was traveling with my husband, scuba diving in Bonaire, and the staff at the resort started using the phase "Blame it on the Venezuelans". For example, if there was a wait of over an hour for lunch or dinner, the staff response was "Blame it on the Venezuelans". It just so happens the Venezuelans flood into United States to go shopping as they transit through the Dutch Antilles resorts for Easter Holiday week.

Because we were diving with Nitrox, an enriched oxygen gas mixture, we had to check our tanks the night before our dive. The tanks we checked were missing the next morning. The dive staff response was "Blame it on the Venezuelans". Evidently, the Venezuelans tourists are also big scuba divers.

This became a constant theme. We have no personal problems with the Venezuelans. This was used as an excuse for anything, bad or inconvenient during our week stay.

Girlfriends, many of you fault someone else for your circumstance. Have you played the victim role? Blaming someone else for your behavior, excusing your inability to take responsibility for your own actions?

Really, we know when we are responsible.

Professional

Girlfriends, we can be emotional. We need love. We need emotional ties with our husband or boyfriend, and also, with other women. Many of us still play the victim, blaming others for a failed relationship, our lack of success or unhappiness. We blame our childhood, our parents, and sometimes even our friends!

Men avoid this trap and see things as they are. They for the most part, take control, and never internalize the situation.

Taking personal responsibility is often difficult. In actually, we are empowered to change our behavior, which may give us our desired results.

Why or what causes a woman not to make these changes? For example, you may think, you want a man, you get him, may become unhappy with your choice, then sabotage the relationship so he leaves. The cycle continues. The excuse is that it was his fault and you blame him for the breakup.

After that, many have difficulty getting on with their life and choose to live in the past. We may convince ourselves that we don't need someone. We may be afraid to take the leap into another relationship, pre-determining that it will end, with an "Oh no, another failure"!

Girlfriends, we can be haunted by past relationships and refuse to move on. Until you are over the hate, anger and resentment you feel, you will never move on.

Only when you process and resolve those issues, can you advance and grow. You can still love a person, yet realize you are no longer in love. The goal is to be "in love".

One sided relationships fail. We all know when that happens. Is there a future with someone who doesn't want to commit? Once your man has emotionally or physically left, you need to move on.

None of us like to be dumped. We prefer to be the dumper. Don't let a fear of commitment lead you into a pattern of dumping a man before you give the relationship a chance. If you do, you will never meet someone for the long term.

Buri (2009) in Psychology Today said this "...have you ever noticed that when it comes to taking responsibility for behavior, people seem to fall into one of two camps...those that are quick to see themselves at fault (I am sorry, it is my fault domination) and those that think it is everyone else fault (lack of self-insight)".

Psychologists' tend to see that women fall into the first camp – quick to see fault in themselves. So what do women do if they see themselves not at fault? They tend to have relationships in which they are critical, discourteous and see the man as a screw-up. Sometimes we fail to engage in self-reflection.

If you are looking to kill the relationship have an affair. If he finds out, it is over for him.

If you want to slowly have it die, use criticism. It will take years, and serve as an unpleasant, lingering death for both of you.

Interestingly, women in their 40-60s tend to exhibits personal responsibility and assume fault more often than women in their 20-30s, who tend to see others at fault.

Girlfriend, the question is "Which are you?" You know when you are responsible! Can you work at changing it?

Self-reflection allows us to examine ourselves, both emotionally and logically. If we can, we may develop a plan and have control over our relationships and ourselves.

Men and women are different. That is a good thing.

Girlfriends, it has have been that way since the time of Adam and Eve. Eve took the first bite, than gave Adam the forbidden fruit to eat. Eve blames Adam. Adam blames Eve.

Perhaps, we, as women, continue to do the same thing. We entice the man and then blame him. He in turn blames us.

How can we stop the cycle?

The first step is to realize what we are doing and the effect it has on our man. Second, we need to change our behavior. Why? Because it will get us what we want. It will help secure a loving and caring relationship with our man.

The man in our life is "perfect" for us. We are "perfect" for him, despite all our faults and his!

XXX. Small Steps to Success as Women…Rub their backs

"I've always made a total effort, even when the odds seemed entirely against me. I never quit trying, I never felt that I didn't have a chance to win" Arnold Palmer

Personal

I was golfing the other day and realized that psychology is a part of sports. No matter how many times over the last seven years I have been golfing, I continue to know what to do and fail to apply it to the game. For example, I hit my irons to the left. All I have to do is move my feet so I hit to the right. I hit my driver to the right and, as you can guess, all I have to do is move my feet so I hit to the left. Yet, year after year I fail to correct a simple habit that will make me a better golfer.

I believe there is a parallel as it relates to relationships.

Girlfriends, we may continue to do the same thing in our relationship or marriage, trying to make major changes, when all that is needed are small, progressive steps. Achieve the small steps and the resultant changes are dramatic.

For example, it may be at bedtime with your children. You rub their back, smooth their hair and they tell you about their day. You learn more in those few moments than you might if you confront them, attempting to make it a major discussion.

It is also true with your spouse or boyfriend. It is more effective to rub their back, tell him you love him, snuggle close and share stories about your day. We need to express our desires and our needs in measured steps to achieve the slow, methodical changes in a relationship, just like I make small adjustments to slowly change my entire golf game.

Professional

I often listen to women and men tell me they have seen a psychologist. They just stopped going, because, during the session, they were asked to do something that was outside of their comfort zone.

For example, one person said he was asked to write a journal about his feelings and he asked, "Why would I want to do that?" Another person was asked to list all the positives about her perceived negatives. She said she was not ready for that. Another woman was having difficulty with her marriage and children.   I asked her to briefly change her focus and do something just for herself. She asked, "Why would I do that?"

It is important for me to remember my undergraduate academic experience. When I decided to get into counseling, my professor told me, that to be empathic, I needed to go to counseling myself.

The session I had with the counselor is still vivid. She said, "Tell me about yourself and what is wrong". I sat silently through the whole session. I wanted to tell her what was going well; how I had attended college in a body cast when my arms and hands were paralyzed; that I did not stay home and feel sorry for myself.

I didn't. My personal experience now allows me to empathize with every new client with whom I meet.

Girlfriends, we know our comfort zone. We know that taking small steps can eventually lead to a big change. The positive relationship changes will come as slowly at the same imperceptible pace at which growing apart occurred.

Each of us handles situations differently. That does not make one right or wrong. It just is.

We approach situations based upon our past experience.

It takes time to have him share and understand your past experience. It may take years. It often evolves through the telling of stories to develop understanding and closeness.

Women need to remember that men don't share their stories readily. Don't be dismayed that it may take some time for him to share all his stories about his past. Listen without being judgmental and by asking too many detailed questions about an occurrence.

Girlfriends, we often want to know everything about our man right up front. If not, we may feel that he is not communicating with us. Don't interrogate or cross-examine him. Just give it time!

XXXI. As Women, we are Strong

"Any woman who understands the problems of running a home will be nearer to understanding the problems of running a country." Margaret Thatcher

Personal

My mom taught me to be strong, to survive and to be independent. She raised me. I know she wanted me to be able to handle any situation I encountered in life, so I could always take care of myself.

My mom was very frugal and from a family of five children. She was raised, post Great Depression, and endured the shared sacrifices of post World War II.

Men plan to take care of the wife and children when he marries. That is his sole drive and is able and genetically programed to do so.

Most women will be strong when we have to be. We know we can pursue life alone or with a man by our side. When the man is not there, we are strong.

I was raised to survive and I can. However, I found out after college, work and my Ph.D. that I wanted more than just to survive. I wanted to share my life with someone, I wanted fulfillment.

Professional

As women, we are strong, like the Spartan women were. When Spartan men were sent to war, Spartan women were left home to take care of the house and finances. More importantly, they were trained in the martial arts to protect themselves as well as their young. They were prepared to stand on their own. Spartan women were trained mentally and physically to take over their duty, until the day they could greet their man coming home from battle.

The modern wife still prepares her husband to do battle in our modern world. If you stop helping him, then he will find someone else who will.

Girlfriends, we need to be strong and prepared. We need to teach and prepare our daughters. Only then, when necessary, we can rise to the occasion. We must be able to meet our daily challenges, until our man comes home!

XXXII. Women Control the Relationship

"My husband tells me he loves me in spite of my job. He does not care where I work or if I do. For me the balance of power is important"
Dr. Wendy James

Personal

My husband learned early on that, when we had a disagreement, he was forbidden to quote my own words from my book. I told him "You cannot use what I write in my book, during a disagreement. You are getting an unfair advantage by getting a look into the female mystique".

Girlfriends, we know we are the ones who control the relationship. Therefore, make sure you earn his love and trust.

Control is different from manipulation. Control is what we do to keep structure and organization in the house, the family and our husband. We make sure things get done and schedules are organized.

I remember when my husband and I were visiting our sister-in-law. She had a schedule on a white board of all the kids' activities, what was happening and when. She pointed at the board and said, she and her husband had no time for each other. My husband took an eraser, went over to the whiteboard and wiped out a kid's activity. He said, "Now you have a free evening". His niece shouted, "You can't do that. It's my pony show".

Girlfriends, you get the idea, we are in control! Therefore, we can use an eraser and make time for what is important in our life. Our husbands do!

My husband is involved with a great group of men and I was getting involved with the wives and girlfriends. He was talking to the guys and they said that, maybe, they could help the women organize. The response from my husband was "Have you even attempted to direct a group of women, it is worst than herding cats. I don't know how they do it, but they find a way of organizing themselves".

Girlfriends, we do like control!

Professional

Death, sickness, injury or money issues can be overcome, if you are strong and maintain control. As women, we can rise to the occasion, whenever needed, whether as a wife, mother, sister or friend.

It is like preparing for battle. Spartan women were physically and mentally prepared and trained in martial arts. Spartan wives were prepared to take over the estate, finances and raise the children.

Reminds me of our military wives. They are ready to take over, while their husbands are at war, and always rise to the occasion.

Girlfriends, we are strong when we have to deal with death, financial situations, sickness and injury.

Men are genetically programmed and able to take care of and protect their wife and offspring.

Once the woman wins the affections of a man, she is the one who controls the relationship. She determines how she is treated, how fast the relationship progresses and all its respects afterwards.

Once the man makes the commitment, defined as marriage, then the woman controls the relationship and demonstrates her strength and proves herself worthy to be at his side.

The woman determines if the relationship stays sexual, exciting, caring, devoted and secure for years to come. It is the woman who makes and keeps the home a place of comfort and love for her husband and her children.

It is the woman and her ability to care and give to her man that keeps him coming home to her at night. She determines the pace, the sexual atmosphere, the love, the devotion and the continuation of the relationship over the years.

Girlfriends, it is a lot of responsibility and work. It is worthwhile, because we get and keep our man.

As a wife, we love our man and make it work! We hold the family together!

Just remember, if you sabotage the relationship, then you have to take responsibility for that too.

No matter how much you disagree, fail to communicate, get angry or upset, the one fact is the commitment that neither of you will permanently leave. One person may go to another room, slam a door, leave the house for a walk or drive around to cool off, yet he/she always returns.

It's important to work through any miscommunication. You know that your man loves and respects you and you love and respect him, beyond all else.

You cannot imagine your life without him in it. That should never be a possibility or a question.

A woman controls the continuation of the love. It is in her hands to keep it going or let it flicker until the flame goes out. Once the fire is out, it will never blaze again. It is over.

It is up to the woman to keep the joy, the excitement, the sexual tension and the love. Also, our man recognizes our strength, intellect and ability to tackle any situation we encounter. We, in turn, encourage and support our husband.

Sometimes, it is work.

It is always worth it! He will love you forever.

XXXIII. Willpower, The Art of Self-Control

"Strength does not come from physical capacity. It comes from an indomitable will"
Mahatma Gandhi

Personal

I determined "Willpower, the Art of Self-Control" was my motivation to move out of the city I grew up in. It is a great city, yet my goal was to work hard, move up the ladder, be able to travel and see the world.

I had a male friend in Kalamazoo, where I was working as a high school teacher. He told me, "You are going to marry a Kellogg cornflake executive, have ten children and look out over the cornfields". Needless to say, I lived in this area. My heart palpitated, my eyes grew big and I thought, "Oh no, he may be right."

About two week later, this same friend and my dad helped me pack up all I could put in my car. The next day, I was on the road driving to Dallas to stay with a college girlfriend and see what was to happen. Luckily, being a teacher, I was paid for the summer. I had the benefit of a few months before I needed income to pay rent.

I moved in with my girlfriend. There were actually five girls living in a one-bedroom apartment.
In retrospect, I cannot remember negatives just positives. Always, having someone there for meals, sleeping on the floor (was no problem), rotating through the bathroom, having our cereal together in the morning was just fun.

After about three months, I had a job. I moved into a two-bedroom apartment with one of the girls. This was luxury living!

I continued to work hard, have goals and was determined to succeed. I continued to move up the corporate ladder. Some jobs worked, some did not, yet, I always learned from my experiences and it led to enhancing my determination to succeed.

Professional

Girlfriends, we need to be motivated and set goals!

We need to have the willpower and self-control to focus and accomplish our goals. The lack of willpower is the most significant barrier to change.

The good news is that willpower is something that can be learned. It directs our lives, eating habits, weight loss, study habits, work habits and spending less time on Facebook and texting.

Willpower is the ability to resist short-term temptations. It is the ability to focus and determine what you want in life and to delay immediate gratification for the achievement of long-term goals. It is willpower that gets you up early in the morning. It is self- control and discipline that allows us to succeed where others fail, regardless of higher IQ's or academic success.

Self-control means no late nights and the realization that you must be responsible. You have a conscious regulation of the self by the self. You are empowered to control your life at work and in relationships. Children with high self-control tend to grow up to be healthy adults.

You determine your own path through life by exercising self-control. It is willpower that drives you along that path in life! Having a positive and energetic personality does wonders too!

You may have motivation and goals yet, without willpower, you may never realize success. Self-control determines your physical and mental health, financial discipline and ability to achieve healthy relationships and pursue your talents to a successful end.

XXXIV. Trust: How do you recover from your husband having an affair?

"The best proof of love is trust" Joyce Brothers

Personal

I have not experienced a lack of trust, because my husbands never had an affair on me. I have dated guys who were sleeping with other women and not just me. I knew that . Thinking about it, we know the signs and choose to ignore them. I did choose to continue to see him, until I found another guy. I realized the guy would be unable to make a commitment.

Girlfriend, just a reminder, if you date a married man, who is disrespecting the marriage? Would you want that?

We always have excuses, "he didn't love her and he loves me, their marriage is over even if he is not divorced". Just be aware a man who is cheating on his wife, even if he divorces her and marries you, will most likely cheat on you too! That is his behavior, and yours too.

Why would you want a guy who does this to his wife? At what point, did we, as women, decide we desire the worst in a man's behavior? Are we not the ones, as women, who make sure men are gentlemen, woo us, treat us with respect and honor us for our love and our accomplishments? Hopefully, as we get older, we get wiser and smarter on relationship issues due to our experiences.

Professional

Girlfriend, trust is a major issue in a relationship.

Women ask me how to recover, how to move on after a betrayal and how to have trust in the relationship again.

I am not sure. You have the very difficult task to forgive, forget and move on. You have to trust him again and that means real trust.

I have found some women, who attempt to "forgive or forget" his behavior, still fail to exhibit trust. They check the house, as they are cleaning, for letters and notes. They check their man's computer, email, and cell phone, if he leaves it at home. That is not an exhibition of trust.

For some women, their man having an affair is about more than another woman. It's about the distance the wife senses from the husband. It is when the husband stays away for longer and longer periods. The husband calls to cancel dinner, because he has a business meeting. Sometimes, it is about another woman and sometimes, it is about the slow distancing, when your man wants to be away from you, rather than be with you.

It may be due, to the inability to connect because of work, children and lack of any interest in the love together. It happens and when you ignore it, then you are in denial.

Now what?

So, yes, I am a psychologist, and I still struggle with clients so they are able to emotionally regain trust. It is also true that most men cannot or do not want to be with a woman they discover is having an affair.

We are in the world of sexting and Internet and other options that take away from the marriage because they focus on a third party outside the relationship. Really, do we want this? Both men and women find even sexting is a form cheating.

Go figure. It is taking away from time with each other by engaging in unhealthy behavior.

We, as women, want to be loved and have attention. If not, why bother marrying? We convince ourselves we are fine with just having sex and do not need an intimate relationship.

Really?

Some women in college indicate they want to concentrate on their studies and just want to have sex with a guy. Yet afterwards, they do not even want to have coffee with him or conversation and definitely do not want to let others know who he is.

College is the one time in your life where you will have a pool of educated, potentially successful men, who you may not find later in the working world, unless you date your boss or your co-worker (neither a good idea).

I find it amazing that many women in their 40-50's, after their children are grown, have an affair, especially those who were "stay at home moms". Something was missing. They found a man to give them attention and sex. They often misinterpreted it for love.

The man might say "I will marry you, after you are divorced". So the woman gets divorced and the guy is in a panic, "Oh no, can't we just be friends, he asks". He had the perfect arrangement of sex with no commitment.

Girlfriends, studies indicate that after three years of cohabitating most guys think, "Why bother getting married?" They have every benefit of a marriage without the commitment.

For some women, having an affair is about her guy becoming distant. His distance may stem from another woman, spending more time at work and slowly distancing himself from you. That can happen in a marriage where both couples have jobs, have the children to raise and become intimately distant over time. That distancing is just as painful, because, as women, we mix up love and passion as one in the same.

So what is the answer?

Girlfriends, we have choices. We can take care of ourselves. 40% of women are the household's primary breadwinners. We can have a marriage, but prefer the man to be at least as successful as we. Otherwise, why bother? We can have love, a career and children. At the end of the day, the question is what will make you happy?

You get to choose and you get to decide. Just choose wisely. You can change you decisions at any time.

Change gets more complicated, when you involve marriage, children, work and feeling like you are taking on all the responsibilities. Remember, your decision is not just affecting you. It impacts all who love and rely on you!

XXXV. Divorce – the slow fading of your bond to each other

"The worst reconciliation is better than the best divorce" Miquel de Cervantes, Spanish writer, author of "El Quijote", 1547 - 1660

Personal

I was widowed but never divorced.

As a widow, you cannot blame the one who died. As a widow, you are lonely and grieve at the loss. In divorce there is a grieving process as well.

There are a myriad of dynamics to a divorce.

There is a 180 degree change from love and marriage to hate and desire for revenge. Sadness and relief are sometimes experienced in equal portions.

Professional

Divorce usually occurs after a slow distancing over the years. Two people fail to recognize the needs of one another and the need for one another. They are forced, by proximity, to interact every day. They are involved together in the house and the children. Somehow, as a couple, they slowly grow apart.

It is like waking up one day and reaching for your love, your "Sweetie Pie", and realizing he is no longer there.

When did the morning hugs, giggles or pokes disappear?

The girl still wants to be a fairy princess. Does her husband still ask her to get dressed up for a night out on the town? Does she dress in something sexy, her fancy dress, the special one she bought and has been dying to wear? Does she still try a new hairdo, add a touch of perfume to her wrists and apply her red lipstick?

When did this end? When did this stop? When did he quit appreciating your efforts? Did you even make the effort?

She reminisces about all those moments, when her husband made her feel glamorous and special. She misses those great evenings out with her man. The music, dinner and wine that used to be so perfect.

When they do go out together and, eventually, arrive home, she finds that the magic has ended. All is chaos.

The children are chasing the dog, the husband goes off to his computer room and the woman stands alone in the middle of the kitchen cleaning up and making coffee in her sexy dress.

Where did the princess go? Where went her prince?

Girlfriends, you know when the magic is gone. The dress is put away, the flannel PJs are put on along with the robe and fuzzy slippers.

Frustration, that things have changed, leads to fighting. It begins about something only we, as girls, remember in the morning.

He has forgotten it by then and is back to his comfort zone, his same everyday routine.

Girlfriend, you know that after an argument is over we cannot resurrect any conversation concerning it, not the next day, the next week or the next year no matter how much we'd like to.

You might want to rehash it verbatim. Believe me, girlfriends he doesn't. Is it really a fight you want to have before your first, morning coffee gets cold? It is not the answer.

Why do the TV shows make marriage look so perfect? Real life is not like "The Waltons", "The Cosbys" or "Leave it to Beaver". We know it!

Those shows portray the woman as the homemaker, the one who is always smiling, perfectly dressed, calm and happy.

Girlfriends, unless he's had an affair, there's plenty of blame to go around in the dissolution of a relationship. Even then, there may be a way to fix it.

Many women think they just want out, because anything is better than feeling emotional emptiness.

Girlfriends, divorce may not be the answer.

The divorce rate in the United States is the highest in the world. Fifty percent of marriages end in divorce. Sixty-seven percent of all second marriages end in divorce.

The good news is there are lots of men to date. They divorce at the same rates too.

The bad news is, with each divorce, the chance of staying together in subsequent marriages diminishes. Unless we learn to do it right the second time, or for us as slow learners, the third, our success in future marriage(s) diminish. Do we really want to go through this painful process again?

As high as these figures are, what is also true is the divorce rate appears to be dropping. The reason for this change is not clear.

Many people cannot afford to divorce. Many people cannot afford to marry. "Baby boomers," who account for a large proportion of our population are no longer in their 20s and 30s, the age when divorce is most prevalent.

The psychological consensus is that divorced life is less satisfying than married life.

Divorce is associated with an increase in depression. When a woman experiences a loss of a man in her life, the confusion and concern about future relationships increases. The change in her lifestyle forces her to re-evaluate previous hopes and dreams.

Girlfriend, realize for a time, you may be sitting in an empty apartment, having to move out of your five bedroom house.

Your children will resent that their lives have changed and blame it on you. It is your fault, even though it's not. You stand alone!

Your married friends tend not to continue to be friends with you and your ex-husband. They do not want to choose sides. They choose to move on and forget about you and your ex.

The financial reality of divorce is often hard to comprehend. The same resources must now support almost twice the expenses. There's no longer a "team" to pull together and combine their incomes.

Girlfriends, it is easy to get out of a marriage. Divorce lawyers are salivating for your business.

It can be pursued in a moment.

Realize that, when the wheels start rolling, hearts turn to stone and both parties are like two dogs pulling on a stick, of which neither will let go. The dogs won't break the stick because they want the whole stick.

Where went that couple, who were so madly in love?

Now they are fighting for every possession they own. They even fight over a toaster oven that has been collecting dust for years. It has no intrinsic value, but now it's worth fighting over?

When you get through it, you may end up sitting in a room all alone and wondering, "Where do I go from here?"

Mentally prepare yourself for this. Don't be surprised. Don't get depressed. Life doesn't end after divorce. It's just beginning anew.

Now what are you suppose to do?

Suddenly, everything you thought was miserable in your previous married life seems better than being alone, staring at the walls. For one thing, it is quiet, too quiet. The sound seems so deafening, so permanent.

Girlfriends, prepare yourselves to be temporarily disoriented. It's a BIG change!

Now, you can call your girlfriends and do what you want to. You may want to have a house again and meet a wonderful man. Make your plans and define your goals for the future.

Some women even want to get back with their ex. Too late! He's moved on. It's just the way men are.

A man will stay with a woman that gives him care, love, and sex. He relies upon us to be at home, raise the children and keep him happy.

Even an abused dog will still wag his tail. He's not wagging out of love, but to avoid more abuse, don't confuse love with avoidance. He will even stay, when he is not in love anymore. For him, it may be enough. For us, it may not be.

The woman controls the relationship. If she starts demanding, nagging, arguing or complaining to him about little stuff, i.e., doing house repairs, sharing in house work, demanding something be done or complaining about him being away, he will stay at the office longer or travel more. Count on it.

He will slowly disappear as husband, lover, friend, father and adoring companion.

The woman will find that she has lost all that she previously wanted so badly and worked so hard to get!

Why do some woman strive so hard to get it all and then casually destroy and discard it?

Girlfriends, when it is over, we get upset and angry. Many of us stay that way and never move on.

Move on!

Life is not fair!

Many will delude themselves into thinking that it was entirely his fault and do not realize that they also must shoulder some of the blame.

Men never feel the same degree of hostility and anger as women do. Men never feel slighted or have their ego damaged by a woman. The man will move on and the woman may pine away for days, weeks, months or maybe years. If you think you'll make him pay and make him suffer, you won't! He doesn't care anymore.

Soon you will be dating. You will find yourself with some additional complications, "baggage"!

Now, you will have to deal with two families. Now it is your ex, his ex, your children, his children, your job and his job.

What seemed like a great idea has turned into another merry-go-round of ups and downs.

You may find yourself in the same situation you were in with your ex-husband, but with more balls to juggle.

If you have not divorced, try to save the marriage.

If it is too late, make sure you plan on what you are going to do and what you want your future life to be.

Can you support yourself? How will it affect your relationship with your children? How will it affect your relationship with his family and your mutual friends? Don't think only of yourself and your unhappiness.

You still control the relationship. The opportunity to resurrect it has not passed.

You have the chance to forgive and overlook his shortcomings. He's probably already forgiven you yours.

Girlfriend, just be aware that it can be lonely out there. There will be no one who cares for you, no one to take care of you and no one for you to take care of. That's the near term reality of divorce.

Your long-term happiness is what you make it!

XXXVI. Getting Old Gracefully

TRUE!

You know you're getting older, when you feel bad in the morning without having fun the night before. - Dr. Wendy James

Personal

I never thought much about getting older, until I was widowed and thrown into the dating pool again.

All of the sudden, life and death issues and getting older were part of my reality. I found myself in my 40s dealing with the death of a husband, elderly parents and the desire to love and be loved again.

One evening, I was out with a group of single, women friends. I was dressing sexier, because my friends told me "no more business suits in the evenings".

I would scan the room at a bar or restaurant and notice women flipping their hair and laughing with their friends, while they surreptitiously searched for eye contact with an available man.

As an older woman, I had more confidence than when I was first on the dating scene. It was a shock to realize I had been married and away from this for sixteen years!

I felt like a stranger in a strange place. Shortly after the death of my husband, I was still in a daze, going through the grieving process, the motion of working, being with friends, meeting new people and learning to be on my own.

I was more concerned with taking baby steps to get through the day. The reality of being in my 40's and single was still something to work through and process.

Today, remarried and in my 50s, I look in the mirror and see the wrinkles and lines. I really want to say that they add character. I realize, though, I am just getting older.

I continue to be alluring to my husband by keeping myself looking good. I do believe I have done a good job of it by exercising and eating right.

Professional

As a professional, I attempt to get women to understand they are going to get older. It's part of the aging process.

Girlfriends, it is going to happen.

It is important to realize, particularly as women, we struggle with getting older. We attempt to fight it every step of the way.

The key is to get older gracefully. Do your best to focus on your passions and interests and learn to play again and enjoy life like you did in your youth. It will keep you young.

As women, we need to make sure we take care of our man. If we are single, we want to look good to attract a man.

Self-doubt is good for women. It gives us the impetus to remain attractive, keep our weight in check, eat right, exercise, pursue our individual goals and keep our man happy.

[handwritten annotation: lost by's long married women / must]

What we need to be concerned about is when self-doubt leads to obsessive behavior. When thoughts such as, "I do not look good enough", "I need to be skinnier", "I need more plastic surgery" and "I wonder if my husband is cheating on me" preoccupy our minds.

Beware!

The problem arises when a woman has lost her self-confidence and feeling of worth. Whether skinny or heavy, she obsesses that her husband needs to love her for her inner self without regard to her physical attractiveness. In doing so, she unconsciously, may be doing even more to destroy her self-image.

Women need other women friends. Make sure your friends are uplifting and provide you with good advice.

Unfortunately, some friends feed on negative thoughts and behaviors. It's true that misery likes company.

Avoid friends who have made negativity the core of their existence. They've given up the good fight and have surrendered.

These negative friends will try to convince us that, no matter what we do, we will be rejected and hurt by a man. Therefore, they try to discourage us from pursuing our dream of seeking a positive and healthy relationship with a man.

The benefit for career women is they know they can financially provide for themselves. Women, who are financially secure, still want to meet a man, so long as he's the one who adds to their life.

For the woman, who does not have a career or has dropped a career to raise a family, there is the danger of focusing on financial insecurities. The pressure to support herself, and, perhaps, her children makes her more vulnerable to entering or staying into a relationship that may not be healthy for her.

Today's environment makes things more challenging. There exists a chance that we can lose our jobs in our 40-50s. At that age, we still have many more years to develop and grow. Many women at this age have children. Suddenly their children are gone and they become empty nesters and are at a loss as to what to do with themselves. Women, reluctantly, realize that the children do not need them anymore. Over the early years, most mothers focus on their children. They may have given up on maintaining and enhancing their relationship with their spouse. If this happens, they grow more distant with their husband. Eventually, they can find themselves alone and isolated.

Often, especially in a divorce, they attempt to make their children their friends or dependent on them, so they are not sitting home alone.

As they age, women, more than men, have the tendency to doubt themselves, their futures and their abilities. We see the winkles, the change in our skin and the change in our looks.

Most men appreciate an accomplished, charming, confident older woman, who is open to engaging in new adventures and experimentation with activities.

Today, with divorce rate hovering around 50%, the fear of being replaced by a younger woman or their man having an affair (a misplaced behavior to boost their self-worth) can cause women to do something irrational. Some women have the one night "revenge" fling. It is not love or passion, but revenge. Does it really make us feel better about ourselves?

Primarily, men tend to define their character, persona and self-esteem through work. A woman defines herself by being a great lover, wife, mother and, if she has one, her career.

Women set the stage for marriage and relationships. Sometimes we get off track.

We are the ones that need excitement, intimacy and passion more than men do.

Men will stay with the women in less than idyllic situations. Men are fairly simple. They are fine if they can come home, have dinner prepared and then retire to the den to get on the computer, watch sports or play videos without us. Girlfriends, we need to be inventive and find things our man wants to do with us or to us!

Girlfriends, we, however, need to be acknowledged by our man through conversation, activities with him, and social events we enjoy do together!

We want to keep busy.

Girlfriends, we are always doing something! We are either working, taking care of the children or helping our friends. We like to be useful and contribute in some meaningful manner. We are the "busy bees".

Sometimes, the intensity of our activity may get out of sync, particularly when our man is ready to slow down or retire. It is so important to have activities you share with your man, so you can be together and have the adventures that were never possible when you were younger. You now have the time and money to do so.

Retirement sounds great! Not having to work everyday is great. Girls, what are we going to do with the time? Have you planned on more special time with your man as both of you retire?

Now, you can fulfill your dreams together.

Have you?

Focus on how you want your life to be.

Get busy. Make it happen.

Be happy getting older, because you have no choice!

XXXV. Dragged into Retirement

"Age is only a number, a cipher for the records. A man can't retire his experience. He must use it. Experiences achieve more with less energy and time" Bernard Baruch

Personal

All of the sudden, something changes you did not expect.

You are dragged into retirement. In my case, it was because my husband was so successful that he could retire early and I was just attempting to take a new direction in my life.

I like to say writing is my second career. Maybe it is just my last stamp on my search to do something meaningful. Maybe, it is just what I do. I need to continue because that makes me the person I am.

My husband sees me as the social person and planned a night of July 4th excitement, dinner, fireworks and meeting new people. He asked me if I needed people and I said "I need people for my stories". Odd answer all around and had me think of what I want in friends.

I realize I get to choose my friends and I do not have to be with those I don't want to.

Girlfriend, how about you?

Oh, this is about retirement. It is about my husband having his time and me having my time and making sure we are together. Yet, that means I need to know what he wants and at what time.

Girlfriends, we always make the guy first. How about the time you canceled a night with your girlfriends to go on a date with him? How about the time you are married and canceled a night out with the girls?

Professional

Women want to make sure we take care of our husband. Suddenly, when he is home with you, it is difficult, because you do not know what time he wants to have lunch. Maybe, he went out with the boys, comes home and wants dinner. You are not even thinking about dinner.

You learn in retirement to communicate in a different way.

He needs his time to chill, sleep in, stay in his underwear and not plan anything. He needs his time to golf, go out with the boys, read, work crossword puzzles or catch up on news.

You are the pleaser, waiting for him. During the day, you go into the den three times to find out when he would like to have lunch. At home or out? For my husband, it is always out.

I just never learned the cooking thing. I have trouble boiling water, until my husband asks, "What are you burning in the kitchen". Usually, it is the teapot that has run out of water to make tea. My husband found the solution, an electronic teapot that shuts off after it is boiling and stays hot when I get around to making hot tea.

After ten years of marriage, my husband asked me "Can you cook anything? I said, "My specialty is the wok and I cannot find it". A few days later my husband found the wok and it is still collecting dust.

When we met, I told him he could pick the room I was going to be good at and he said the bedroom. I sighed in relief, because I never have cooked.

Sometimes I wait by the door for him to come home. Often, I am immersed in my own activity, usually writing or researching.

Girlfriends, all we want is to love and please our lover. And yes, you have to have your time to find something or a place where you can do what you are good at!

So now girlfriend, my husband knows he cannot manage me. As a result, I bought him a dog and he manages the dog. That has worked out just fine. The dog sits at his feet, gives her sad look, cocks her head and listens to him.

Retirement is bliss. You just have to work out the balance things. I need attention, nights together and nights out with other couples. And I want him to golf with me! Now, we have figured out how both of us can have pretty much what we want.

Reminds me of the time my husband and I were in Hawaii. Two little girls were with their parents at the Ritz-Carlton in Maui. The three year old came over and crawled into my lap. The six year old stood next to my husband and looked at him, as we were eating shrimp cocktail. My husband asked the six year old, "What do you like best about being a kid?" She thought about it, took her time and responded, "I pretty much can do anything I want to and I don't have to work" My husband said, "That is exactly what I am trying to do and it is called retirement".

XXXVI. Commitment: Marriage is special and sacred

"Sometimes winning is about making sure the other person fails to win by denying them their ability to win. They lose and you win by default. That is not a marriage. Marriage is trust, love and honesty" Dr. Wendy James

Personal

I love being married! I love sharing my life with my husband!

I know he will be there for me through the good times, the bad times, in sickness and in health.

When you are happily married, you are with the man of your dreams. It is your responsibility to make sure he lives his dream. It is his responsibility to make sure he supports you in yours.

My husband is the first one who is proud and excited about my accomplishments. He is the first one I call and run home to at night to share my day! When I have a great day, I do the "happy dance" and he knows my adrenaline is pumping and lets me have my moment!

Girlfriends, who can you depend on to be there for you? For some, it is their husbands. When we are growing up it is usually our mother and father. Why? It is because usually our mother and father who want us to succeed and are there for us. It is about family and bloodlines. You know they will always be your family. As I ask my friends, "Who will be there for you when you are old and your parents have passed away"?

I am not attempting to diminish the importance of girlfriends. Yet, once a girlfriend meets a man or marries him, he is first in her life and is supposed to be.

I married and I ended up going to all my girlfriends and telling them, my husband is now first in my life and I will not be going out as often to the bars or happy hour with them. I would see them for lunch, dinner or the occasional girls' nights out.

No, you cannot have close guy friends. No, your husband cannot have huggy-kissy girl friends. It just does not work. Chemistry happens between one sex and the other and jealousy may occur. Girlfriends, avoid it!

Many young women asked me, "Why do I need to be married? Why can't I just live with him?

My answer is always the same, "Marriage is a commitment that makes it work".

Marriage is about commitment. Marriage is special and sacred. It is a special bond that does not happen when you live together. Most important is to realize why you are together. You may both share a relationship with God. God gives us strength and leads us to marry a person with the same values, morals and character. I have to talk about God and marriage, because belief in God is what allows us to care and give, as husband and wife, unselfishly and through the good and bad times.

Girlfriends, you trust and believe that your husband is there and will not leave. You know you can trust him and if he breaks that trust, or you his, it is the worst thing that can happen. Love and trust make a relationship! Selfish behavior fails to make a marriage. We are all human, yet, girlfriends, when we say to him, 'Do not do it again", we trust he will do so and so will we.

I told one of my girlfriends I would do anything my husband asked me to do, because, if he asked, it was very important to him! I would honor his wishes. Guess what, my husband has never asked me to do something such as relocate or take a new job. If he did, I would say, "Yes". How about you? Do you have that much trust and love for your man?

Professional

Today, there is an increase with couples living together and never getting married. Statistically, if you are living together for more than three years the chances of getting married diminish greatly. Why would the man bother? He has everything he would want in a marriage, without the commitment.

There is the fact that the National divorce rate is over 50%.

It's good news for those looking for a man, bad news for those in a marriage, who may lose theirs.

Are you making your marriage a win-win or a win-lose situation? To make a marriage a win-win you have to mange it to a win-win conclusion. Why would we expect anything less in a relationship?

What about you?

There are the articles about women having sex with no emotional attachment. In fact, the men they "hook up" with do not even want to talk to them or have coffee afterwards.

Really?

Women, why do we allow men to text us for a date or through Facebook? Is that a relationship? I think not!

There are the studies that show that 40% of women are breadwinners today. Why do we need a man? We can support ourselves.

Girlfriends, today we have options! More women, as a percentile, are more educated then men. More women are getting Masters and Ph.D's than men. Most women do not want to be with a man who is not at least as successful as they are. Otherwise, why bother?

I find men desire successful and intelligent women. You have to have something to talk about or adventures to reminisce about after sex. We just have more options and freedom than we used to.

We can choose! Yet, choosing means having an honest relationship with your husband. We get to share our thoughts, our days, our happiness and love with the one we love, honor and trust 100%.

Made in the USA
San Bernardino, CA
29 November 2013